LION IN THE
WHITE HOUSE

LION IN THE
WHITE HOUSE

A Life of

THEODORE ROOSEVELT

AIDA D. DONALD

BASIC
BOOKS

A Member of the Perseus Books Group
New York

DESIGNED BY JEFF WILLIAMS
Set in 12-point Adobe Caslon

ISBN-13: 978-0-465-00213-9

Book Club Edition

For my family with love—
David, Bruce, Jenni, Aleta, Maia

It is not the critic who counts. . . . The credit belongs to the man in the arena, whose face is marred by dust and sweat and blood; who strives valiantly . . . who knows the great enthusiasms, the great devotions; who spends himself in a worthy cause; who at best knows in the end the triumph of high achievement, and who at worst, if he fails, at least fails while daring greatly.

—THEODORE ROOSEVELT

Introduction

We were following Teddy. . . . We had been ordered to
retreat before that, but it wasn't authenticated. Teddy didn't
pay any attention to it anyhow. We went ahead and started
up the hill. We got everybody together—cavalry and some
infantry. . . . We went up the hill . . . it was wide open. We
didn't run in a regular line. . . . It was just like a mob going
up there. . . . We were exposed to the Spanish fire. . . . Roosevelt went on and overran the trenches, and he was maybe
seventy-five yards ahead of us—he was always ahead of us.

THIS IS HOW A SEVENTEEN-YEAR-OLD
trooper in Theodore Roosevelt's Rough Rider
regiment described his leader.

In this account, as in all other stories about Roosevelt—
and there were scores over the years—he "was his own
limelight," as the novelist Owen Wister, who knew him,
acutely observed. An incandescent figure, by the age of
forty he seemed invincible, with his jutting jaw, too-large
teeth, gleaming eyes, spectacles, and a muscular body

poised like a cat ready to strike. A steam engine of a man, he had already established a reputation for himself in multiple, and overlapping, realms: writer, cowboy, politician, environmentalist. Now he added soldier. Soon enough, he would add president and world leader to the list. In every realm he mastered whatever task he took on. He was, quintessentially, a reformer in a turbulent age.

Roosevelt was the most popular man in the country when he was president and was the most renowned world figure by the time he retired. Realizing this extraordinary man has always been a challenge. Perhaps it is best to think of his story in three dimensions: the man himself, the national leader, a world leader. The dimensions, happily, allow for a narrative that is chronological.

Roosevelt was born into wealth and position in New York City in 1858. As a child he watched Abraham Lincoln's bier pass by his grandfather's mansion in 1865. The martyred president became Roosevelt's hero and silent mentor in his public life. He often referred to him in explaining his positions to Republicans and others. During his severest trials, Lincoln was his touchstone.

When he was a boy, Roosevelt was sickly, and how he transformed himself into an athletic and confident man is the stuff of legends. By his twenties, his daunting frame housed an immense intellect and literary talent. His father loved and encouraged him and sent him to Harvard, where he picked up a scientific and secular outlook that guided him in his multiple interests as an adult. On graduating from college, he married the romantic love of his life, but after an idyllic three years, he lost her in childbirth. He gave his infant daughter to his sister to raise and fled to the West to recover from his devastation.

At twenty-three years old, Roosevelt had decided to become a politician, not a usual gentleman's profession. He was elected to the New York State Assembly three times but was thwarted as a reformer. When he returned from the West, after two years of mourning, he picked up his public life, so strong was his call to public service. His sojourn out West, however, was forever imprinted on him. Later, he would make many more trips there. He became a rancher and an early and prodigious environmentalist.

Roosevelt married his dear childhood friend, Edith Carow, in 1886. During the early years of their marriage, he combined his government work with a career as a writer. He alternated between writing ordinary biographies for income and true masterpieces, such as *The Winning of the West*, which made him small fortunes. He became a civil service commissioner in Washington for six years and then police commissioner in New York City for two years, serving in both posts as a reformer cleaning up corruption. He then became assistant secretary of the navy, where he built a modern American fleet. When war with Spain over Cuba seemed imminent in 1898, Roosevelt resigned to be lieutenant colonel in a regiment he formed called the Rough Riders. He quickly became a heroic warrior in a short and profitable war for America. At forty years old, he was the master of men and a shaper of destinies.

That "splendid little war" made Roosevelt the popular candidate for governor of New York, despite the fears of Republican Party bosses that he would be independent and too reformist. He was a progressive in his outlook, and he made it clear during his campaign that he intended to improve the lives of working men, break up business monopolies, sever the malign ties business had with political parties, and make the judiciary sensitive to reformist legislation.

As governor, he was a moralist and brilliant manipulator of publicity for causes. He was a magician, too, in his use of the bully pulpit. Roosevelt exhorted the people and government officials to be virtuous. He was sufficiently successful that his tenure in Albany became an apprenticeship for the presidency. New York's Republican boss kicked him upstairs to get rid of him. After a brief stint as vice president, he became president when William McKinley was assassinated.

At forty-two years old, Roosevelt was the youngest president in history. His political career, jump-started by a war and hailed by progressives, was astonishingly swift. His ability to bring together high character and purpose attracted Americans. His ebullient and joyful persona entranced voters. Roosevelt brought his country back into the light of the future at a time when the nation most needed it. The sense of high purpose that had mobilized the country during the bloody civil war was now nearly lost. Americans were being diminished and demoralized by a heartless laissez-faire economy that seemed to serve only the industrial barons and financiers.

Roosevelt's presidency of little more than seven years, from 1901–9, was the high-watermark of Republican progressivism, national reform, and international success. He refashioned the office of the chief executive and reordered the Republican Party to achieve his ends: the reform of business practices and the empowerment of labor. He broke business trusts to open up economic opportunity to all, mediated strikes, made food and drugs safe, and preserved the environment—and much else as well. In foreign affairs, he added the Roosevelt corollary to the Monroe Doctrine to keep European imperial powers at bay. He built the Panama Canal and rebuilt a powerful navy to secure the country. And he played peacemaker in European and Asian wars, winning the Nobel Peace Prize, the only sitting president to be so honored. He led the nation out of isolation and made it a part of the roiling world that needed a strong and impartial peacemaker.

Roosevelt was the only progressive president in the history of the Republican Party. In fact, Roosevelt's presidency was one of the great forward, or progressive, eras in the nation's history as a whole. His party never again reached such heights in advanced legislation or in the care of the people. No Republican president since has embraced the idea of creating, through active government, the greatest good for the greatest number of people.

His years in office had the makings of an imperial presidency, but that was an extension never imagined by Roosevelt. He believed the chief executive had all the powers not forbidden by the Constitution, but these should only be exercised in the service of positive government to further opportunity for all and to defend the nation through strength and within a world system.

Roosevelt's legacy was enormous, and it found a home, a generation later, in his cousin Franklin Roosevelt's Democratic Party. Within his own Republican Party, his influence was short-lived, as the organization quickly fell back onto its usual track of conservatism and small visions. Never since has the Republican Party put forward such imaginative and responsive domestic policy initiatives. And only recently have Republicans renewed their interest in international affairs. As they struggle for mastery abroad, Roosevelt's only mild foreign interventions, reasoned uses of military power, and attachments to communities of nations challenge their perceived lessons of the past.

CHAPTER I

Born in a Cocoon

When I was four years old . . . I bit my sister's arm. . . . I . . . remember running down to the yard, perfectly conscious that I had committed a crime. From the yard I went into the kitchen, got some dough from the cook, and crawled under the kitchen table. In a minute or two my father entered from the yard. . . . My father immediately dropped on all fours and darted for me. I feebly heaved the dough at him, and, having the advantage of him because I could stand up under the table, got a fair start for the stairs, but was caught half-way up them. The punishment that ensued fitted the crime, and I hope—and believe—that it did me good.

I was a sickly, delicate boy, suffered much from asthma, and frequently had to be taken away on trips to find a place where I could breathe. One of my memories is of my father walking up and down the room with me in his arms at night when I was a very small person, and of sitting up in bed gasping, with my father and mother trying to help me.

When I was a small boy I began to take an interest in natural history. I remember distinctly the first day that I started on my career as a zoologist. I was walking up Broadway, and as I passed the market to which I used sometimes to be sent before breakfast to get strawberries, I suddenly saw a dead seal laid out on a slab of wood. That seal filled me with every possible feeling of romance and adventure.

THESE ARE THE EARLIEST MEMORIES OF Theodore Roosevelt, as recounted in the autobiography written when he was fifty-five years old and at loose ends, after a tumultuous and history-making life. Three elements are prominent in these recollections—his challenge to authority, the care his father gave while tending to his life-threatening illness, and his attraction to nature's wonders.

Theodore Roosevelt, Jr., was born on October 27, 1858, in New York City, the second child and first boy in what would be a family of four children. He weighed eight and a half pounds and began life as a hearty baby, bright and hyperactive. His mother remarked that he looked like a terrapin, but he was soon declared a beautiful child, blond and blue-eyed. His family called him Teedie. By the time he was three years old, he was suffering from bronchial asthma, which gave him a special place in his father's affections—none of the other children was so severely ill—and dogged him almost all of his life. When nothing else could make him breathe at night, the little boy was bundled into the family carriage, and father and son raced over cobblestone streets to jostle Teedie's lungs into action.

Teedie was born into an old, rich, and aristocratic family. His father was the youngest of the five sons of the wealthy Cornelius Van Schaack Roosevelt, a Dutch merchant prince and real estate entrepreneur in New York City. The elder Roosevelt's fortune was estimated at five hundred thousand dollars, a considerable sum when laborers could earn a mere fifty cents a day. Little is known about this ancestor, except that he was very rich and that Dutch was still spoken at his dinner table. He gave all his sons houses in then-fashionable neighborhoods upon their marriages. Teedie's father received a simple brownstone with a yard at 28 East Twentieth Street, between Fifth Avenue and Broadway. It was furnished "in the canonical taste" of New York, Roosevelt remembered, "the black horsehair furniture in the dining room scratched the bare legs of the children when they sat on it. . . . The middle room was a library, with tables, chairs, and bookcases of gloomy respectability. It was without windows, and so was available only at night. The front room, the parlor, seemed to us children to be a room of much splendor, but was open for general use only on Sunday evening or on rare occasions when there were parties."

A magnificent chandelier of cut-glass prisms dominated the room. Once, Roosevelt recalled, one of the prisms fell from it, and he stowed it away in "furtive delight" as a treasure, although fearful that he would be caught and "convicted of larceny." It was a "marvelous" ornament, a delight that the little boy knew must be kept secret, as he would sometimes keep other pleasures hidden.

Teedie's father, Theodore Roosevelt, Sr., was the major influence on the boy. A sixth-generation New Yorker, he was exuberant and powerful, an impressive-looking lion of

Theodore Roosevelt, Sr. (Greatheart)

a man with abundant dark hair, a full beard, and piercing blue eyes.

The senior Roosevelt had married Martha Bulloch, a southern belle from Georgia who was called Mittie and was a great beauty, with translucent skin, lustrous hair, and a fine figure. But she was fragile and often sick with headaches and stomach ailments. Able neither to run a

Martha Bulloch Roosevelt (Mittie)

good household nor to raise her children, Mittie left those burdens to a very willing husband. Teedie was oblivious to his mother's domestic and maternal deficiencies, for Mittie was affectionate and playful with her children.

As a couple, Mittie and Thee, as the senior Roosevelt was known, provided an example to their children of an exceedingly loving marriage, although one in which the father was dominant and the mother dependent. Their relationship imprinted a pattern of family dynamics on their elder son.

Teedie was a homebody as a very young boy, whether in the city, on vacation in the Adirondacks, or at Oyster Bay, and he preferred the country, where he could go barefoot, play at being a cowboy or an Indian, or even at being a farmer, doing all the seasons' chores.

Teedie's neighbor in the city was his unconventional uncle, Robert B. Roosevelt, a lawyer who also wrote novels. Robert was a political reformer and conservationist. He contained in his persona a multitude of interests and was part of the large Roosevelt clan, remaining so despite the fact that, years later, he kept a mistress while being married. Young Roosevelt was undeterred by Robert's eccentric ways. When he thought he wanted to be a lawyer, he sampled the profession in his uncle's firm. Family loyalty remained uppermost in the Roosevelt universe. And as a child, Teedie learned much from his uncle: Robert's writing interest, his reform temperament, and concern for nature were his gifts to his nephew.

Teedie was alert to politics at a very young age. He knew that his mother wore her politics on her sleeves in the epochal Civil War years. She was a Confederate sympathizer and remained "unreconstructed to the day of her death," or so he recorded in his autobiography. She clung to her family, with its Old South values—the Bullochs held slaves and were staunch Confederates—even in the face of her husband's Republican and antislavery views.

Papa Roosevelt supported the Civil War as an effort to restore the Union and free the slaves, and he was a fervent Abraham Lincoln Republican. Lincoln's political and eco-

Theodore Roosevelt, Jr. (Teedie) at 18 months

nomic programs appealed to Thee. He regarded the president's call for free labor (slavery would not be extended into the territories and would ultimately end), infrastructure improvements, a sound banking system, the establishment of colleges, and more free land in the West for settlers as reformist and farseeing.

In the seesaw politics of the Roosevelt family, Teedie sided with his father and used his mother's apostasy to his advantage when in trouble. Roosevelt wrote that once, as a small child, while awaiting punishment by his mother for a transgression, he defended himself by praying out loud for the success of the Union army. His mother was "too much amused to punish" him. (His father, however, admonished him for his stratagem.)

Mittie's Southernness in no way diminished the boy's love for her. His salutations to her in letters written in later years tell of an almost romantic attachment. They ranged from "My darling Mother" to "Darling Little Motherling" to "Darling Muffie." He called her "the sweetest little mother that ever lived." The Cavalier in Teedie was tucked in securely, although he was a Yankee.

Mittie taught Teedie her family history, stripped of its darker side of being dis-Unionist. She dwelled on how the Bullochs had fought in the Revolution. In those days, one Bulloch was in the Continental Congress and another served as governor of Georgia. In the Civil War, a brother was a celebrated Confederate naval officer. Mittie made sure that Teedie knew that Sherman's troops had trampled the Bulloch plantation and even looted the house.

Mittie's stories very much overbalanced what Teedie learned of his Northern ancestors. A Roosevelt had been a New York senator and an ally of Alexander Hamilton in the battle for the Constitution, but there was little high drama beyond that. The commercial, nonmilitary Roosevelts—the family owned and operated a flourishing business importing plate glass for buildings in a fast-growing city—hardly matched the agrarian Bullochs for heroic and martial exploits. It would be hard to overestimate the importance of the lessons of the Civil War on the little boy who loved history, action, brave deeds, and large causes.

Teedie admired his strong, protective father, and he strove to emulate him as an alpha male. His deep and loving attachment to Thee that began when he was an ailing boy developed into a heroic view of his father as he grew older. Teedie developed into a son who always wanted to please his father. He set high expectations for himself and never wavered in his pursuit of praise from his father.

The senior Roosevelt was a celebrated man in the already great city of a growing nation, who enjoyed the comforts New York held for the rich and cocooned his family from its poverty and crime. In the 1850s, the city was not unlike the London of Charles Dickens with its dirt and destitution. Teedie's city counted almost one million residents, most of them ill-housed, in want, and subject to the terrifying booms and busts of business cycles. In the uncertain world of getting and losing, the poor formed the largest class.

Papa Roosevelt made philanthropy his real work in spectacular and highly publicized undertakings. He was a pious Christian and an elder of the Presbyterian Church—he left the Dutch Reformed Church to worship with his wife—and he followed the teachings of the social gospel, which obliged the followers of Christ to help the poor. You served God by helping your fellows. Of the many examples Papa passed on to Theodore, this one, perhaps, was paramount.

He created institutional safety nets for the children of the poor, for orphans, for the sick and the disabled. Over the course of his life, he helped to establish charities, including the Children's Aid Society, the New York Orthopaedic Dispensary and Hospital, Roosevelt Hospital, the Bellevue Training School for Nurses, and the Newsboys' Lodging-House. He supported the Young Men's Christian Association (YMCA) and was interested in improving the House of Refuge for Orphans and two insane asylums. His wealth allowed him to be an entrepreneur in large, private charities. Historically, charity was administered by local governments or churches, but they were always stingy and stigmatizing. These old ways could never meet the enormous challenges introduced as high capitalism created masses of laborers who were poverty stricken and often ill, badly housed, and unable to take care of their children. The senior Roosevelt tried another way that was robust and long-lived, until the twentieth-century welfare state emerged.

Other Roosevelt philanthropies were broadly cultural. Papa helped establish the Metropolitan Museum of Art and the Natural History Museum, later called the American Museum of Natural History. With other rich men who were Republicans, he established the social Union League Club, an elite society. It unexpectedly took on a political cast after the Civil War and became a fortress and refuge for Republicans in Democratic New York City.

Roosevelt set an example for his family of a patrician helping a less fortunate class. You aided the masses but kept your distance from individuals. Papa only sometimes visited the young homeless newsboys. On rare occasions he took his children to his philanthropic charities to acquaint them with a bit of the other side of life. It is arguable whether these visits made an impression on the children, although Theodore and his sisters, at a later age, followed the tradition of noblesse oblige.

Papa Roosevelt did not pass on to Teedie and his siblings either a personal connection with the poor or empathy. When traveling in Italy, for example, he beat a beggar child bothering his family. On another day, father and son threw a basket of cakes to hungry and destitute women and children. Teedie especially enjoyed the escapade, as he lobbed cakes into hungry mouths. It was as though the Roosevelts were at a zoo.

The paternal example was central in the lives of the Roosevelt children. Papa's good works were reflected in the shorthand of family sayings long remembered: Man is not an oyster; cowardice and deceit are not tolerated; affection and a hopeful disposition are rewarded; get action, that is, seize the day. The patrician reformer never conceived that only a central government would be rich and powerful enough truly to help the poor or that social and economic conditions themselves needed change. That private charity could only ameliorate conditions would be revealed to his son a generation later. The ultimate failure of patrician philanthropy, earnest and generous, was that it could not diminish poverty.

Papa Roosevelt was his young namesake's greatest hero. He let down his junior only once, when he bought a substitute to fight for him in the Civil War rather than take up arms against his fragile wife's brothers in the Confederate services. Theodore Jr. recorded that his father was "the best man I ever knew," but he added that he "was the only man of whom I was ever afraid." Yet only once was Teedie reprimanded. So powerful was an admonition from Papa that no Roosevelt child sinned a second time.

The children were cocooned at home for schooling. There were four Roosevelt youngsters—Anna (called Bamie, for the Italian *bambina*, or baby), Teedie, Elliott, and Corinne (Coni)—and their close friend, Edith Kermit Carow. At first, Teedie was tutored by his aunt, Anna Bulloch, in a little class with his siblings and Edith. What kind of picture did this little grouping of youngsters make?

Teedie was a spindly little boy with large teeth, light hair, and blue eyes. His sister Anna wore a brace because of spinal trouble, a kind of tuberculosis of the bone which later made her a bent figure, and Corinne suffered from asthma, although family records do not show it was ever as serious as Teedie's. Elliott had seizures.

The tutees enjoyed their lessons, but they were mostly entranced by Aunt Anna's great tales of the Bulloch family's brave military role in the Revolution. She reinforced the glorious exploits also being taught to Teedie by his mother. These martial tales mesmerized the tot who soon developed a love of adventure books. One of his favorites was David Livingstone's *Missionary Travels and Researches in Southern Africa.*

About the same time, Teedie became interested in natural history, and he even began to keep a copy book, or diary, of observations. He was a curious and playful little fellow by age seven. He often put frogs under his hat, letting them leap out as he saluted friends on the street, dropped snakes in water glasses at the dinner table, and hid odd creatures in the icebox. Teedie was always ready to be delighted by nature. In his autobiography he recalls the first time he was beguiled by science. He was eight years old and running an errand for his family when he came upon a dead seal "laid out on a slab of wood." He proceeded to measure it on the spot, and the budding zoologist later did some research on seals' lives and habitat.

The romance of science was like a light bulb Teedie awakened to. Mostly he studied birds. At ten he wrote in his diary, "Today, we went down to the brook. But wonders were in store for us. It seemed as if all the inhabitants of the brook had got down to one point. In a small pond that has an island in the middle of it. At that place we saw crayfish, eels, minnows, salamanders, water spiders, water bugs etc. etc." He inexpertly described other findings: "We found a swallows, catbirds, and robin nests. . . . The robins and catbirds nest I pushed from limbs with sticks. We knocked down two pair of birds nests but did not take them. All of a sudden we saw high in the barn and with a wasps nest near it a swallows nest. We got it with a ladder."

An observant Teedie was becoming an amateur ornithologist and natural scientist. He would soon learn how to stuff birds and keep them in what he called a museum in his bedroom—which also contained many other small creatures—along with scientific instruments and smelly chemicals. Sometimes little creatures ran free or slithered around, so scaring the maids that they refused to enter his bedroom. He boasted, at age eleven, of having a thousand scientific specimens adorning his room. In a few short years, Teedie had advanced from reading about nature's creatures to hands-on scientific activity and writing. He wrote natural histories, including one on the seal, as well as "The Foraging Ant" and "The Natural History of Insects," the last when he was nine years old. When he was fourteen, Theodore asked to be allowed to wear glasses, and the colorful, buzzing natural world suddenly became clearer to him. Finally he could see well all the wonders he had already discovered in nature. Teedie had also developed a keen interest in reading serious history. Undoubtedly fired up by his family's tales of military valor, the boy read widely and especially liked James Fenimore Cooper's stories of frontier life and Captain Frederick Marryat's tales of the sea.

Theodore Roosevelt, Jr., at 11 years old

In 1868, Mittie suggested to her husband that it was time to expand the children's horizons by exposing the youngsters to other civilizations. So the Roosevelts went to Europe when Teedie was ten years old, staying for about a year. Teedie recorded in his diary that he didn't learn very much.

He kept a full travelogue of sites and activities, but he had no context—historical, emotional, psychological, or aesthetic—to judge their value. Interspersed in his diary are notations that he was homesick: "I cried for homesick-ness and a wish to get out of the land where friends (or as I think them enemies) who can not speak my language are forced on me." When it came to foreign travel, he was probably like most ten-year-olds.

Teedie almost morbidly chronicled his bad health, as though it were as permanent as having an arm or leg. In his diary he records frequent bouts of illness—asthma, stomach ailments, and headaches. Yet he also shows that he was al-most always willing to go on hikes with his father or to join the family riding out to historical or architectural sites. He was a game little boy, although he almost always paid a heavy price after any strenuous activity. In one stretch of his European trip, an overactive Teedie recorded being sick for a day or more just about every week. Foreign doctors treated his illnesses and tried different medicines. Some-times, when he had an asthmatic attack and could not breathe, his father gave him a cigar to smoke or his mother rubbed his chest. Mittie turned out to be an incompetent masseuse, but Teedie was outwardly uncomplaining, recording in his diary only that "I was rubbed so hard on the chest this morning that the blood came out."

He encountered the next milestone in his life when he was twelve. He was still puny and gawky, an indoor boy who read a good deal and did so standing with one foot pulled up, rather like a stork. It was more than his parents could bear. His father built a gymnasium on the second floor of their house to encourage athletic endeavors, having already built an outdoor piazza to allow his children to play outdoors all year. Papa's much-recalled admonition to Teedie was, "You have the mind but not the body. You must make your body." It was the beginning of the young Roosevelt's lifelong campaign to be fit and manly.

Theodore developed his chest and arm muscles by lifting dumbbells, by using the horizontal bars, and by bashing a punching bag. Then, his father was inspired to give the boy boxing lessons, and boxing became important in his maturing life. His pugilistic talents were a source of his combativeness at genteel Harvard, out West when he met ruffians, and in the White House, where he loved to challenge martial friends.

When Teedie was thirteen, his father brought in a tutor who taught the little family circle French, German, and Latin. French was spoken at the dinner table to encourage fluency. In his later life, Roosevelt's use of French surprised diplomats, who had not known an American president since John Quincy Adams to speak a foreign language. Theodore was not fluent but he could read German.

In the fall of 1872 the family went abroad again, but this time to the strikingly different Middle East. Teedie, almost fourteen years old, was ready for adventure and learning. He blossomed. He not only grew an inch or two, and needed all new clothes, but he became healthier. His diary shows that he appreciated the cultural life spread before him—the soaring cathedrals and golden mosques, the beckoning cities, the grand architecture, the lost civilizations, and the matchless, almost fantasy world of Islam.

He was also developing a new style of writing. Many diary passages are romantically descriptive, precise, and informative. He wrote on November 28, 1872, "How I gazed on it! It was Egypt, the land of the dreams; Egypt the most ancient of all countries! A land that was old when Rome was bright; was old when Babylon was in its glory; was old when Troy was taken! It was a sight to awaken a thousand thoughts, and it did." The next year Teedie rhapsodized about the palace of the sultan in Constantinople as "one of the cheerfulest yet one of the most beautiful palaces" he had ever seen. It was "composed of marble, verd antique, porphory, precious woods and inlaid with Mother of Pearl. In some of the rooms were massive silver ornaments representing tigers fighting with horses, attacking zebras and stags, pelicans and crane[s] by stre[a]ms etc." Teedie's descriptive powers, observations, romantic inclinations, openness to differences, knowledge, and flights of imagination even at fourteen display an emerging gift as a writer. Along with his sheer joy in the use of words and in the wonder of human accomplishments, they would develop to make the best of his mature history irresistible.

CHAPTER 2

From Cocoon to the World

I do not think there is a fellow in College who has a family that love him as much as you all do me, and I am *sure* that there is no one who has a Father who is also his best and most intimate friend, as you are mine. . . . I shall do my best to deserve your trust.

———————

Remember me to Annie and Fanny, and give my love to Edith—if she's in a good humour, otherwise my respectful regards. If she seems *particularly* good tempered tell her that when I see her at Xmas it will not be on what you call one of her off days.

———————

I have been living in a perfect dream of delight. . . . We are having an ideal honeymoon, and the dear little wife can rest all she wants to, and is the sweetest little dor-mouse that ever lived.

ON THEODORE'S RETURN FROM THE MID-
dle East in 1873, the new Roosevelt mansion
at 6 West Fifty-seventh Street, off Fifth Avenue, was ready.
Papa Roosevelt built it with some of the inheritance he received after his father's death. It was extravagantly and ele-
gantly furnished and was altogether like a little palace. It
shouted his great wealth to the world.

Now fifteen years old, the well-traveled and confident
Theodore was readied for Harvard College by a new,
special tutor. He became the different child in the family,
the only one to seek a higher education. That he wanted
to be a scientist mandated university studies. He was an
apt pupil. He favored history and modern languages, but
he also studied Greek, Latin, and mathematics, finishing
his preparation in two years instead of the usual three.
After he had breezed through his eight Harvard en-
trance exams, his self-esteem was undoubtedly puffed up
so high as to float him into his college. His tutor laconi-
cally recorded that his mind had "an alert and vigorous
quality."

By the time Theodore entered Harvard at age eighteen,
he had reinvented himself. He discarded his early view of
himself as a little ape, with skinny legs and a thin body
holding up a large head that seemed mostly teeth. He had
reached his adult height of five feet eight inches and
weighed 130 pounds; his chest measured thirty-four inches
and his shoulders forty-one. Now he saw himself as a stur-
dier, more combative boy. He had tremendous energy; he
could ride, shoot, pole-vault, and do the hop, skip, and
jump. He was totally self-possessed, knew himself well,
and never had an identity crisis.

Roosevelt dressed as fashionably as the young gentlemen around him and asked his college classmates to call him Ted. He had long ago dropped Teedie, and he disliked Teddy, which only his first wife later called him. His appearance had a roundness and a ruddiness. His hair was wavy and brown, and he sported long sideburns. They were undoubtedly intended to make him look more manly, but the choice to wear them is puzzling because facial hair, so characteristic of Civil War soldiers and politicians and the heroic look, was becoming passé.

Ted was popular at Harvard. He was an enthusiastic and knowledgeable conversationalist, had a delightful sense of humor, and was more than outgoing in his new environment. Some of his friends later recalled that in odd moments he could be bumptious and overbearing. They record no particular incidents, only his aura. It seems that when Ted could not control his overenthusiasms, he was an unpleasant character.

Theodore was clearheaded in mind and spirit. In keeping with the age, he was secular and scientific; his religious side emerged only for his Sunday churchgoing and Bible teaching. He was very accurate in observing life and had acquired almost total recall. His writing skills, developed over years of diary keeping and small writings, were considerable at a time when such skills were almost totally lacking in Harvard College undergraduates.

He fit in at Harvard, which was an upper-class institution. His speech, with a broad *a* and a softly trilled *r*, showed that he was a part of the elite of the Eastern seaboard, which shared a distinct culture of speech, language, education, and behavior. These wealthy families formed a caste later called the Establishment, which dominated the country in Roose-velt's years and later.

Theodore chose to live off campus—at 16 Winthrop Street in comfortable rooms furnished by his older sister, Bamie—so that he could concentrate on his studies and treat his asthma, if it came upon him. That illness, how-ever, seemed to diminish as he grew older. He spurned the commons for meals and made private arrangements, even joining a dining club of the best Bostonians. He ate vora-ciously at all his meals. His breakfast, for example, could include tea or coffee, pancakes, and a beefsteak. Because he took a lot of exercise, he stayed trim.

Theodore followed the line of least resistance in choosing his social circle. He was a snob and was taken in by the other snobs at Harvard and in Boston. Bamie, who summered in Newport with Brahmins, opened doors for him, too. The oldest and moneyed families of Saltonstalls, Cabots, and Lees, among others, welcomed him to weekend parties. Soon enough, he was squiring beautiful girls of impeccable lineage, galloping around stately ballrooms (he never learned to dance well), going on idyllic picnics, joining skating par-ties on scenic ponds in the winter, and generally keeping a social calendar of frenetic activity. Theodore reported much of this to his family and added that he did not pay much at-tention to New Yorkers because he did not know them. When Theodore left his cocoon, he chose to be a Boston butterfly.

Enchanted by the natural world, he hoped to become a scientist. His early years of birding, of shooting and stuff-ing birds, of smelling and of being stained by strange chemicals, and even of being disheveled by living in the forest or in his home laboratory in his bedroom, all pointed in this direction. As usual, he aimed high, as he hoped to emulate the great naturalist, John James Audubon.

Crucially, Ted's father approved of his scientific ambitions in his freshman year. He told Theodore that he had made enough money so that his son did not have to work for a living. He then gently laid out the near and far consequences of his son's choice. Theodore had to be serious in pursuing a scientific career and not be a "dilettante." As his son summed up the lesson, "If I went into a scientific career, I must definitely abandon all thought of the enjoyment that could accompany a money-making career, and must find my pleasures elsewhere."

So, in the greatest age of men amassing and passing on immense fortunes, as the Roosevelts did, Theodore chose the life of the mind. He was going to continue to be the original in the family, the boy and man who carved out his own path, different from his siblings or the other rich sons of his class. He would satisfy his innermost desires and drives at Harvard, which was undergoing its own metamorphosis under President Charles W. Eliot.

Eliot took over Harvard College in 1869 and was turning it into a university in the German model of learning centered on research and a new kind of teaching. In the judgment of a Harvard historian, he transformed a "fashionable finishing school" into a modern university. Theodore's scientific bent, inner discipline, and seriousness were a perfect match for this new, exciting educational experiment. Before Ted arrived in Cambridge, Eliot had publicly laid out what he had in mind. He wrote that "Universities are teachers, storehouses, and searches for truth." Furthermore, he said, "A university . . . has . . . a unifying influence in regard to political discussions and divisions."

The president's new educational goals included changing the students themselves. In effect, he seemed to want to make them more like what the young Roosevelt was at age eighteen for, as Eliot put it, he wanted to shift "external compulsion and discipline" in learning to "internal compulsion and discipline." The students had to want to learn, as did young Roosevelt. Eliot poked at the lazy and spoiled Harvard boys to wake them up to the new challenges of the age. Roosevelt was already wide awake.

Of his Harvard College experience, Roosevelt wrote in his autobiography, "I thoroughly enjoyed Harvard, and I am sure it did me good, but only in the general effect, for there was very little in my actual studies that helped me in my after-life." Roosevelt also jotted down that he "saw almost nothing of President Eliot."

But Ted may have been recollecting an Eliot who would become an adversary when Roosevelt was president. Ted took the heady atmosphere around him for granted. He did not comment on whatever improvements were being made, which ultimately ended a fixed curriculum and rote learning and replaced them with electives, new fields of learning in the sciences and liberal arts, Socratic methods, and essay writing. Ted seemed oblivious to Harvard's history and Eliot's intentions. When Eliot made brilliant new hires to put the college in the forefront of knowledge, Roosevelt left no insightful record. For example, the soon-to-be-famous psychologist and philosopher William James joined the faculty. James, whose training was in medicine, taught Theodore anatomy. Surely some early flourishes of his famous work on Pragmatism, one of his great contributions to philosophy and psychology, would not have been left in the wings as he lectured. Theodore took history with

Henry Cabot Lodge, a good historian who was writing books and, significantly, would soon be Roosevelt's mentor and great friend when he gave up science for history and politics. Lodge encouraged Theodore's love of history and writing and gave him an inquiring view of America's continental expanse and the nation's debt to the first settlers. Then there was George Santayana, already a great scholar and philosopher.

Roosevelt could have been the poster boy for Eliot's university. But when Harvard made laboratory science, and not natural history, the center of the science curriculum, Theodore soured on a scientific career. He did not want to be indoors as a "microscopist" and "section cutter," he recollected, but outdoors with faunal nature. Also, a scientist needed at least three years abroad for study. During his junior year he was becoming attached to a Boston girl who frowned on a long stay in Europe.

Whatever his reasons for giving up science, the young man was stranded at a critical stage in his education. Then, too, Ted found college an unknown world beyond academics, which were a breeze for him. Usually, he had to puzzle out harder things, such as how to earn the esteem of his teachers and classmates. His way was sometimes unfortunate, for he tried to dominate both by speaking out of turn. A famous story has Professor Nathan Shaler, one of Harvard's eminences in natural history, admonishing him, "See here, Roosevelt, let me talk. I am running this course." We don't know the subject of the contretemps between them and have only the recollection of Shaler's outburst from one of the students. Theodore was also brash in James's course, continually arguing with the august professor. James, however, was merely bemused by the outspoken student and gave him an honors grade. Theodore could not help but always try to be the center of attention.

He met social challenges in a martial spirit. He boxed at Harvard, was put in the lightweight class, and advanced to the finals in one competition. He lost but was upbeat about his performance. His courage won the admiration of his friends. What was probably as important, he had passed a test, a rite of passage toward acceptance and manhood.

Theodore was an earnest student at Harvard, despite his father's advising him that his studies were third in importance after taking care of his morals and health. He set himself to a rigid schedule of study and in his first year was a B student, which was then, as now, considered an ordinary ranking. His average for the seven subjects he studied—Greek, German, Latin, classical literature, physics, chemistry, and mathematics—was seventy-five when the passing grade was fifty. He received honors grades in five subjects; mathematics and Greek proved very difficult.

A successful first year at college behind him, he went on to greater things in the summer. He published his first writing, a pamphlet on the summer birds in his beloved Adirondacks, where his family fled each year from the fetid streets and foul air of New York City. He was happiest living close to nature. After considering all the small creatures he had observed for so long, Theodore chose as his favorites the small, winged, colorful animals whose lives he then captured in print. He was also a talented sketch artist as a naturalist and embellished his writings—from his diary to his scientific writings—with his drawings. But this first book on birds was only a scientific catalogue, simply written. The study showed that he was

Theodore Roosevelt, ca. 1877,
in sculling togs at Harvard College

probably outstanding for his age and accomplishments in
natural history.

Theodore hit his stride as a student in his second year
when he studied languages, sciences, and history. With his
apparently photographic memory as well as his drive and
enthusiasm for knowledge, he earned honors grades and
compiled an average of eighty-nine, putting him in the top
tenth of his class.

The spur to Theodore's high academic performance, however, was trauma. In 1878 his father, the lion of the family, or Greatheart as he was called, died of peritonitis. He was only forty-six years old. The death sent Theodore into a maelstrom and wrenched his whole family from its emotional moorings.

The family was convinced that Papa Roosevelt had died from disappointment. He had been dipping into Republican politics but had not gotten far. Greatheart had become a famous reformer, an independent-minded Republican, and that sank him twice with the politicians who ran the Republican Party. He had just been denied the greatest patronage plum under Republican control, collector of customs in the port of New York, a post that made both the holder and the party very rich. Earlier he had been spurned by the New York legislature for a seat in the U.S. Senate. (Senators were not popularly elected until 1917.) The high and low politicos at home and in Washington wanted only men who took orders. While at home for his father's funeral, Theodore, who was more scientific in his judgments than his family, quietly marked his father's rejections as despicable political acts. He kept them close and in the forefront of his mind.

The senior Roosevelt had told his namesake before he went off to college that he was his favorite child, and junior never lost his immense love for his father. After his death, Ted's private diary is full of anguish. The boy was devastated. His father "was everything to me," he wrote. One historian suggests that Theodore's "sensitivity" was "so extreme" that it "veered on mental imbalance."

Theodore tried to remain cheerful in letters to his family in order to keep up everyone's spirits. But he shaved off his whiskers and returned to Harvard mature overnight. He had become the head of his family, and all his life he tried to look after it. He would be like his late father and he never forgot him. Years later, when Theodore dined with his two sisters on his first evening in the White House as president—he had not yet moved his family to Washington—he would wistfully wish that his father could be present to witness the momentous occasion.

Back at Harvard, and more serious than ever, Theodore maintained his grade average and class standing through his third year. In two subjects, philosophy and natural history, he placed first. Then his spirits lifted a bit when he was tapped for the Porcellian Club, the top social group at the college. Theodore was a big man on campus his final year at Harvard. He was an officer of the Porcellian Club, in the Hasty Pudding, the Natural History Society, and the secret societies, which had names like A.D. and O.K. He was also the editor of one of the three undergraduate newspapers. His three-year average of eighty-two ranked him nineteenth in his class. He tested well, in the nineties in two classes, and he won honors in almost all his courses. He also wrote a senior thesis on equality for women, in which he favored granting suffrage to them if they wanted it. Why he chose the subject and came to his conclusion remain mysteries. He seemed philosophically open on the question. Maybe politics really interested him now that science was receding. Later, as a politician, he was cautious about implementing women's suffrage.

In an astonishing writing endeavor, one outside his Harvard studies, Theodore began a naval history of the War of 1812. Why this war, this topic? The Bulloch family's naval experiences, so well known to him from his mother's tales, made him think that if the Confederacy had a stronger navy it might have fared better. Such a notion also surely originated in the dark experience of the United States in the War of 1812, when presidents and politicians refused to prepare to defend the nation by building a navy during the perilous time of the Napoleonic wars. Navies just had not seemed important in America's wars. The Napoleonic wars, however, showed otherwise. The powerful Napoleon had challenged Great Britain's great navy, and it had defended England from invasion. In contrast, because the United States did not have an effective navy to protect its shores, in the War of 1812 the British invaded the country, burned Washington, and ravaged the land at will. Roosevelt bundled together the inadequate Confederate navy and the Jeffersonian/Madisonian experiences of not being prepared for war. He became a naval proponent at an early age.

The writing exercise thoroughly engaged Ted intellectually and for some years, until he finished and published his book. Perhaps, all along, he was testing himself about being a historian. He vastly admired Francis Parkman, and if he chose to be a historian, he wrote, he wanted to reach the same heights. Still a tyro, he was sampling history, along with science and politics, in his capacious mind.

THEODORE'S SOCIAL RELATIONSHIPS with young women were shaped by the comfortable experiences of his home life. He loved his closest woman friend, Edith Kermit Carow, and had been emotionally attached to her even as a boy. Then, when he was in Europe at age ten, he recorded in his diary how much he missed her, and he signed letters to her, "Your loving friend." When Theodore was nineteen and Edith was seventeen, something happened to their relationship that is unexplained. Family members claimed in later years that Theodore had proposed marriage and Edith had spurned him. Then it was recalled that the two dearest friends separated because they were temperamentally unsuited. Theodore's self-confidence might have grown into impetuosity, while Edith's bookish demeanor had matured into a levelheadedness. Perhaps they were too close to each other, in a kind of brother-sister duality that should not lead to marriage.

Theodore recounted the painful episode to Bamie in 1886: "Edith and I had very intimate relations; one day there came a break for we both of us had . . . tempers that were far from being the best. To no soul now living have either of us ever since spoken a word of this." But that was in 1886, and it was meant to inform a beloved sister about a clandestine relationship.

Whatever the deep truth about his youthful infatuation, Theodore stalked away from Edith after their quarrel. He was so distraught that he went off on wild rides on his horse and even shot a neighbor's dog for a small transgression. Aside from the personal hurt he undoubtedly suffered, it is the first recorded episode of how violently Roosevelt could behave when he was thwarted.

In the fall of 1878, Theodore met the romantic love of his life. She was seventeen-year-old Alice Hathaway Lee, of an old and wealthy Boston family, a relative of one of his classmates. The romantically impetuous Theodore fell instantly and madly in love. Alice was, according to contemporary sources, an "enchanting creature" of "singular loveliness," "quick intelligence," "endearing character," and "unfailing sunny temperament." She was "gay," exceptionally "bright," and "the life of the party." One historian calls her "a ravishing beauty" who bedazzled all around her and Theodore. "A firestorm of passion" consumed him, the historian concludes.

Alice's family thought her too young to be serious about any boy, and she continued to play the field. Nevertheless, Theodore was relentless and made another of his precipitate proposals of marriage. Alice declined. Theodore would not accept another rejection. He openly pursued Alice and even tried to get other boys to stop paying attention to her. Once again, his behavior tended toward violence. He considered challenging one persistent suitor to a duel. Theodore was determined. Not quite whistling in the dark, he revealed to a friend at a party, as he pointed to Alice, that he intended to marry her, even though she would not have him.

Theodore pursued Alice for months with all the ardor he could muster. After the false start of wanting a strong and independent wife, he chose a girl like his mother, the woman his heroic father had chosen years before. Roosevelt senior, Theodore's beau ideal of a fully realized man, had married the fragile and ethereal Mittie, and Alice seemed a carbon copy. Certainly, in appearance, Alice and Mittie were alike. Alice was a five-feet-seven-inch beauty with gray eyes and brown hair that looked golden in sunlight.

In Theodore's campaign for Alice's affection, he sucked the air out of any pretensions others had for her. He showered her with romantic attention and immense affection at parties, teas, and outings. Finally, Alice realized how much Theodore loved her and how much she dared love him. She agreed to a secret engagement of a year.

Alice Hathaway Lee Roosevelt

In June 1880, Theodore graduated magna cum laude and Phi Beta Kappa from Harvard and was ranked twenty-first in a class of 177. (He said he began college in a class of 230 boys, and some sources put the figure at 246.) All in all, he had an excellent record, even considering that many of his classmates were fops, more interested in social than intellectual life. (Perhaps only one other twentieth-century president—Woodrow Wilson—matched Roosevelt's academic achievements.)

Theodore was twenty-two, and the world was his oyster. He was a college graduate and engaged to a splendid and wealthy young woman. And he himself was rich. His father had willed him $125,000, or an income of eight thousand dollars a year. (In New York City the average family lived on four hundred dollars a year.) But Ted was already showing signs of careless management of his resources. He had more money in his last years at college than the average Harvard boy, and he had bought his fiancée a too-costly engagement ring. He demonstrated that he did not use his wealth wisely, a problem that would have consequences later. Still, at the time, his future looked dazzling.

On his twenty-second birthday—October 27, 1880—Theodore and Alice were married in the Unitarian church in Brookline, Massachusetts. They took a quick honeymoon (they would go to Europe later), and then the young couple moved into the Roosevelt mansion. Theodore enrolled in the Columbia Law School and also read law in his Uncle Robert's firm. Seemingly, he had found a vocation. He often ran the miles to the school and back each day, continuing to meet each new challenge with energy.

Theodore, however, soon grew disenchanted with the law. Only later did he explain, more than once in letters and writings, that he found the law lacking in social justice and only a cover to protect wealth and business. It was a critical judgment, made early in life, which would soon carry into a turbulent political career. He dropped out of law school before his second year was out; he was ready for a total change. He would look for a profession in which he could make a difference, one that would totally engage him and burn up his immense energy. He would wrestle this new world bare-handed.

CHAPTER 3

"I Rose Like a Rocket"

The people I knew did not belong to the governing class. . . . I intended to be one of the governing class. . . . I certainly would not quit until I had made the effort and found out whether I really was too weak to hold my own in the rough and tumble.

The party was still treated like a private corporation, and in each district the organization formed a kind of social and political club. A man had to be regularly proposed for and elected into this club, just as into any other club. . . . I had to break into the organization with a jimmy.

I grew to realize that all that Abraham Lincoln had said about the Dred Scott Decision [the Supreme Court decision in 1857 that denied freedom and citizenship to an African-American slave whose master had brought him into a free state] could be said with equal truth and justice about the numerous decisions which in our own day were erected as bars across the path of social reform, and which brought to naught so much of the effort to secure justice and fair dealing for working men and working women, and for plain citizens, generally.

WHILE STILL IN LAW SCHOOL—WHEN HE dropped out later, he would read law for a while in a private firm—Theodore decided he would be a politician. In his letters he recorded that he rejected a life of leisure, for he thought men ought to do some kind of work. He was aware that, all around him, rich men engaged in philanthropy, literature, science, or business. But politics suited his temperament and ambition. It would fuel his abundant vitality and need to be on the go and make things happen. For a gentleman, his career choice was not idiosyncratic. He had already learned some hard political lessons from his father, and he had imbibed enough patriotic history from Henry Cabot Lodge, his mentor at Harvard, to inspire him to service. He had also acquired a scientific outlook, although he did not ever connect this attribute to his politics. Collecting facts, observing firsthand, and deciding by reasoning were scientific contributions to his political arsenal, yet he seemed unaware of their source.

Roosevelt aimed to restore the old virtues and programs of the earliest Republicans. He staked out his philosophy of government, and his political tactics were aggressive and energetic. The party ought not only to be brought back to reform, to fair dealing for all who worked, and to social justice for all, but also the best men ought to lead in the struggle. They needed to seize the Republican Party from low achievers and corrupters. The Republican Party and its presidents shamelessly preferred only to advance big corporations whatever the cost. Big business lavished funds on Republican leaders, especially those in the Senate, to run the country. As a result, there were scandals and there were weak and bewildered presidents. The executive branch was in eclipse. Roosevelt thought himself something of a reformer, after his father's model, a person who leads to clean up government through civil service reform and legislation. He would make himself the different drummer in the Republican orchestra. His mentor would be the martyred President Lincoln, whom he saw as honest and reforming. He would grasp the mantle of Lincoln's legacy and began to stud his speeches and letters with Lincoln's wisdom, philosophy, and politics.

Roosevelt began his political life at the lowest possible level by joining the local Republican club in the district (now Manhattan) where his family resided in New York City. It consisted mostly of lowlifes who wondered what this well-dressed youngster was doing at their meetings, especially when he sometimes showed up in his dinner clothes. (Roosevelt always dressed for dinner.) The cigar-smoking, spittoon-spitting Republicans, although amused, saw an opportunity. They wanted to appear to be reforming in the Twenty-first, the silk-stocking, District. An intraparty fight threw over the usual hack Republican holding the seat, and Roosevelt won the nomination. What could they lose by giving this upper-class Harvard man in dinner clothes a chance to be elected by his own kind? Theodore, who partied with the likes of the Vanderbilts, Dodges, Astors, Harrimans, Jays, and the Fish family, would be seen in the election as a man who could not be bought, who was a fighter, and who could rally the rich to his side. He did not need a jimmy to get into the Republican Party, as he colorfully wrote in his autobiography. Rather, he was a political wedge in intraparty politics. Just as the Republican leaders hoped, the city's wealthy men backed Roosevelt with enough money to make a good show. Men like the financier J. P. Morgan and the lawyers Elihu Root and Joseph H. Choate rallied to the cause. Roosevelt ran a Mr. Clean campaign. He would rid the city of human and real garbage: the reigning Republican assemblyman in his district and the manure and detritus piled in the streets that threatened health and safety.

In getting out the vote, Roosevelt was a human steam engine in a pince-nez, and he constantly stressed his distance from party bosses and corrupt interests. He would be independent in local affairs, he asserted, but a loyal Republican at higher levels. His Democratic opponent was the recently fired director of the local insane asylum. Roosevelt won, garnering more than twice the normal Republican vote. With exquisite manners, he wrote to one of his wealthy backers, "I shall endeavor to do my work honestly."

When Roosevelt took his seat as assemblyman in Albany on January 2, 1882, at just twenty-three years old, he was the youngest member of the body and the oddest character the lounging men had ever seen. Without a topcoat, dressed in a purple waistcoat, he had raced to the capitol on a frigid day. That evening at the party's caucus, he showed up in a formal cutaway coat with tails and carried a high silk top hat. He sported a gold watch and fob and a gold-topped cane. The sartorially splendid Roosevelt had a round, ruddy face, ample brown hair parted in the middle, and thick, reddish sideburns. He seemed all teeth when he opened his mouth. Some colleagues sniggered that he was a Knickerbocker dandy. Early on, when he was challenged by a bully, he met him with "I hear you are going to toss me in a blanket. By God! If you try anything like that, I'll kick you, I'll bite you. I'll kick you in the balls. I'll do anything to you—You had better leave me alone." Roosevelt's voice was high and geeky, but his streetwise language struck home. He was never bothered again.

Almost immediately upon entering politics, Roosevelt noticed how businessmen and politicians worked together. He was not antibusiness and was, in fact, a probusiness legislator at first. But he wanted a clean relationship between business and politics. They were separate activities. Furthermore, some business practices and some political practices needed to be changed, to be reformed for the benefit of all people. He turned to his uncle, James Roosevelt, the Hudson River aristocrat and influential Democrat (father of Franklin Delano Roosevelt, who was to marry Theodore's niece, Eleanor), for advice about the sordid legislative arrangement, but James only tried to acclimatize his nephew to the prevailing practices of the day: go along to get along. Republicans were supposed to use their power to advance business interests. How they went about it disturbed Roosevelt. They often blackmailed businessmen by threatening to pass bills that would be detrimental until they were paid off.

Theodore was not willing to be led down that crooked path. For him the bedrock of politics was morality, and business practices that bilked citizens were immoral. Looking back at those times in his autobiography, Roosevelt wrote that "honesty . . . and decency . . . and administrative efficiency are the prime requisites for a legislator."

Roosevelt was elected into a Democratic assembly. He knew how hard it was going to be to get anything virtuous done. He was put on the cities committee and, working with a few reformers, introduced bills to clean up the city's water supply, to reform the election of aldermen, and to defund the city's sinking fund, which was a sum of money set aside to pay back the city's debt and was a honeypot for corrupt politicians. And he tried to get the overburdened court of appeals some relief. All he accomplished, however, was a watered-down bill on aldermen, although it was later seen as an achievement.

Roosevelt made a noisy and mighty effort to impeach T. R. Westbrook, a justice in the state supreme court, because he was in cahoots with the incomparable corrupter Jay Gould in a railroad swindle. The *New York Times* had exposed the sordid case, but Westbrook protected Gould's financial interest despite the law, the Constitution, and morality. Gould was a "shark" of capitalism, Roosevelt thundered, to the astonished delight of the reformers in the assembly. His resolution of impeachment was tabled, as an old warhorse of the system attacked him. As reported in one account, he bloviated about "that dude," Roosevelt. "The damn fool . . . would tread on his own balls just as quick as he would on his neighbor's." That evening, Roosevelt was almost lured into a trap to assault him. A prostitute feigned an injury and sought his help, but he put her in a cab and sent a police detective to the woman's address, where he learned that thugs were waiting for him. Politics was not beanbag in Albany. It was violent and personal. Then, because it had been paid a bribe, the Westbrook investigative committee, just before the end of the session, recommended against punishing the judge. Worse, the assembly approved its decision. After this and other political atrocities, the legislative body was labeled the most corrupt since the halcyon days of Boss Tweed and his henchmen, who bilked the city out of tens of millions of dollars.

While waiting for the denouement of the Westbrook case, Roosevelt dealt with other affairs. He showed an unreformed attitude toward labor in bills in the assembly and opposed a minimum wage of two dollars a day for city workers. Then, despite his opposition and that of others, a bill passed to raise the salaries of police and firefighters to make them equal to those of other city workers. Roosevelt thought he was protecting the city's treasury, but he was out of step with his closest reforming friends. As yet he had developed neither sympathy nor understanding of the state of laborers in the battle heating up between them and capital in the rising industrial economy. Then Roosevelt had an epiphany. For a bill to outlaw the making of cigars in the filthy tenements where mostly immigrants lived—a bill he initially opposed—he publicly announced his change of heart. He had visited the wretched of the earth and had seen with his own eyes the conditions in the industry. The social horizons for the swell living in a mansion had been permanently stretched. How the other half lived staggered his imagination.

Roosevelt's second term in the legislature was a revelation because his thumping on desks, bellowing "Mista Speaka" to get attention (sometimes for forty minutes), and introducing mostly reformist bills—certainly those pertaining to business and government—made him a candidate for speaker of the assembly. But he was buried in the avalanche of a Democratic resurgence as the opposition took the assembly, senate, and governorship. To Roosevelt, the honorific was nice but empty. Minority leaders had no power, except as nattering birds.

Grover Cleveland, the new Democratic governor, was a reformer and, surprisingly, called on the Republican Roosevelt to do something about the spoils system that was more than blemishing democracy. Cleveland wanted civil service reform in the state government; that is, he wanted to replace the buying of jobs with a merit system based on examinations. The U.S. Congress had already acted in 1883 with the Pendleton Act, which placed about 10 percent of federal jobs under civil service, and Cleveland wanted New York to follow suit. Roosevelt had already introduced such a bill, but it had languished in the judiciary committee. Cleveland wanted it brought to the floor for a vote so that reformers of both parties would join to pass it. With these men united, the assembly agreed, after a long struggle with the Democrats, and the senate swallowed the poison before adjourning. Roosevelt was as much a father to civil service reform as was Cleveland, and he always thought it was his signature accomplishment as an assemblyman, although he actively worked for reform in many other bills that came his way. He was still the boy legislator, but he showed himself to be a man honing a set of principles and leading a band of reformers—progressives who were the independents in both parties. He was viewed as a politician with a future.

Roosevelt was exhausted after the legislature was adjourned. That summer he suffered a serious illness from his old troubles, Alice was pregnant, his rising Oyster Bay mansion with its twelve bedrooms needed attention, and his finances were in a mess. He was living beyond his means.

Assemblyman Theodore Roosevelt, ca. 1884

Roosevelt won a third term in the assembly, as Republicans swept back into office in both houses. When the assembly organized itself for the 1884 session, Roosevelt was not voted speaker. Unbelievable shenanigans deprived him of the leadership he had earned, but he won good committee assignments, and his friends did, too. All was not lost, although the battle showed that the young tyro was not the

Republican leader in the state and had made enemies of the suspicious, nonreforming elements in the party.

In retrospect, Roosevelt probably had scared the traditional Republicans with his intemperate opposition to the Five-Cent Bill in the last session of the assembly. Most wanted to cut the fare on Jay Gould's elevated railroad line in Manhattan. Not only was Gould making a great profit, he was also evading taxes. Roosevelt led the attack, but he was so full of piety—one journalist thought Roosevelt had a pulpit under his pants—and so outlandish in his speech that he startled many Republicans when they were not joining the Democrats in great horselaughs. It was this speech, however, that made Roosevelt the prince of invective. He said that Gould and his partners were "common thieves . . . they belong to that most dangerous of all classes, the wealthy criminal class." Cleveland, a stickler for constitutional niceties, vetoed the bill.

Roosevelt had been equally harsh on politicians. At a mayoralty election, he favored a candidate "who will treat the tumors of the body politic with the roughest and most merciless surgery. . . . We want a man who will put in the knife fearlessly," he had roared. Furthermore, Roosevelt had charged that the city's politics were run by "an oligarchy composed of demagogues, officeholders and corrupt party wirepullers." He had already taken on the role of a modern Sisyphus.

Roosevelt dedicated his third term in 1884 to cracking the party machines and investigating corruption. He introduced three bills. One would raise the beer tax. A second was intended to give some fiscal discipline to the state. A third tried to give power to the mayor of New York City and reduce the aldermen to bystanders. In a fierce struggle,

Roosevelt got his way on two of the bills but not on the beer tax. Then he was appointed chairman of a committee to investigate the corruption in New York City. In fits and starts, with bursts of Rooseveltian invective at city employees, he persisted in the investigation for weeks. Roosevelt introduced a blizzard of bills, while his main investigation piled up thousands of pages of testimony. Many bills passed, reforming aspects of state policies, but Cleveland vetoed many others. Roosevelt would not be denied. He persevered.

And then, while Roosevelt was battling corruption in Albany, his private life in New York City came tumbling down. He was summoned home by the dire news that both his adored and pregnant wife and his beloved mother were desperately ill. He rushed to his mother's house on Fifty-seventh Street, where the young couple had moved for Alice's confinement, only to watch helplessly as Alice died in his arms of kidney disease after giving birth. Mittie, meanwhile, succumbed to typhoid fever. Roosevelt was devastated. He gave his infant daughter, Alice Lee, who was named after her dead mother, to Bamie to raise. It all happened in the bleak month of February in 1884.

A year later, he was able to face the reality of his loss in a tribute to Alice that read, in part:

> I . . . loved her as soon as I saw her sweet, fair young face . . . . We spent three years of happiness such as rarely comes to a man or woman. . . . Fair, pure, and joyous as a maiden; loving, tender, and happy as a young wife; when she had just become a mother, when her life seemed to be but just begun, and when the years seemed so bright before her—then by a strange and

terrible fate, death came to her. And when my heart's dearest died, the light went from my life forever.

Once Roosevelt made his peace in words with his cruel fate, he never looked back. He firmly shut his tender lost love and its memory from his life forever. He did not think he would ever marry again, for he was opposed to second marriages, and he reorganized his life as a bachelor politician, outside the city and with greater means than before. From his mother's estate Roosevelt inherited $62,500. He sold his house at 55 West Forty-fifth Street, and it was at this dark moment that he speeded up building his new and permanent mansion at Oyster Bay, Long Island, on the many acres of land he had bought earlier. He had planned the house the summer before in anticipation of the large family he and Alice had hoped to raise there. They would call it Leeholm after Alice's name, but now he renamed the large and sprawling house Sagamore Hill. It would be his homestead and retreat for the rest of his life.

After a well-attended double funeral in New York City, Roosevelt returned to the Assembly, where he received overwhelming sympathy from his colleagues. His private world shattered, he threw himself into politics. He became increasingly attracted to the rewards and hazards of a wider political life and went to the Republican national convention in June 1884, where movers and shakers were choosing a presidential candidate. Roosevelt backed a reformer, but James G. Blaine, probably the most corrupt of all the available Republican politicians, was chosen. A continuing battle marred the selection, as the Stalwarts, the old party faithful, were pitted against the Independents, the reformers like Roosevelt. He held his nose and supported Blaine. He made it known that he was not going to get involved in the murderous war between the two wings of the party and repeated his mantra that he was just a Republican, "pure and simple." He was, and would remain, an independent politician. Of course, his moral stance put him at odds with the New York Republican bosses, who now had even more evidence that he was untrustworthy.

After the Republican convention, Roosevelt was depressed and weary. He decided to go west for the summer and before the presidential campaign heated up, when he would return and give some pallid campaign speeches. He thought that, if he moved fast, Black Care might not catch up to him. For at least a part of his life, he would be a Westerner. He was a divided man, with one foot in the East and one in the West. He built a ranch house in the Dakotas and bought more cattle. He already had four hundred head, which he had bought for fourteen thousand dollars, grazing on government land, as was the custom. Earlier, when Alice indicated that she did not share his Wild West enthusiasms and would not live in the Badlands, even for short periods, Roosevelt had stalled in his western dreams. But now the bachelor cowboy restarted his western engine. Before too long he would invest eighty-five thousand dollars in cattle and buildings near the Little Missouri River. At first he was a financial partner in the Maltese Cross ranch at Chimney Butte. Then he became the owner of the Elkhorn ranch.

Over the next two years or so, during his stay in the West, which was broken periodically by forays to the East for family or other needs, Roosevelt fell in love with the country of vast horizons, incredible natural architecture,

Theodore Roosevelt in Dakota Territory, 1885

abundant wildlife, and huge and remarkable animals. He described the open prairie as having a curious and fantastic beauty of its own. He wrote that before it became "the isle of ghosts and of strange dead memories, it was a land of vast silent spaces, of lonely rivers, and of plains where the wild game stared at the passing horseman." He experienced perfect freedom as a cowboy and hunter. But he took revenge on the land for his misfortunes in the East. He killed scores of animals in a kind of orgy of violent easing of his tensions. Hunting was an ordinary activity of westerners, but Roosevelt seemed beyond normal.

Some of the most vivid stories that began to give Roosevelt a mythic quality come from his western experiences. He was his own public relations expert and portrayed himself as a cowboy. Next to being a soldier (which for him would come later), the cowboy was popularly considered the nation's most manly occupation. That he was really a rich rancher who employed cowboys did not seem to matter, for he lived and worked like a cowboy. He willingly and eagerly shared the hard life of the ranch hands, ate dust, lived in the saddle sometimes for forty hours straight, and rode hard. He admitted he was not the best of horsemen, knocked down a ruffian making fun of his wearing eyeglasses, and fought cattle thieves, among others. Roosevelt became exhilarated. He was a man's man in a man's world. More significant, for the first time in his life, he was living in equality with a class of men beneath him in the social hierarchy. He liked them, and they returned his affection in lifelong friendships. He became gregarious and earthy.

Roosevelt's writing about the West to friends and family centered, at first, on colorful incidents in his everyday affairs. That he was to create a new version of himself as a western cowboy was probably not intentional, but his ability as a storyteller led to his creating a great myth about himself. In one story he told how he had tracked three crooks, caught them, and, after days of travel, handed them over to the law. Roosevelt was a deputy sheriff at the time. His instant and breathless recountings from Dakota to his friend Henry Cabot Lodge were almost stream of consciousness (more polished versions appeared later):

I got three horsethieves in fine style. My two Maine men and I ran down the river three days in our boat and then came on their camp by surprise. As they knew there was no other boat on the river but the one they had taken and as they had not thought of our building another they were taken completely unawares, one with his rifle on the ground, and the others with theirs on their shoulders; so there was no fight, nor any need of pluck on our part. We simply crept noiselessly up and rising when only a few yards distant covered them with the cocked rifles while I told them to throw up their hands. They saw that we had the drop on them completely and I guess they also saw that we surely meant shooting if they hesitated, and so their hands went up at once. We kept them with us nearly a week, being caught in an ice jam; then we came to a ranch where we got a wagon, and I sent my two men down stream with the boat, while I took the three captives overland a two day journey to a town where I could give them to the Sheriff. I was pretty sleepy when I got there as I had to keep awake at night a good deal in guarding, and we had gotten out of food, and the cold had been intense.

Roosevelt immersed himself in western surroundings and folkways. Despite his dudelike, fringed buckskin clothing, eyeglasses, and fancy locutions like "hasten forward there" spoken in a squeaky voice, he was a cowboy. But he was always the keen observer, too, of an unknown and fascinating land. He often seemed more at home in the rough than in a plush, eastern environment. He was that unusual aristocrat who knew the continental United States as well as the cramped but civilized cities of the eastern seaboard. He wanted to introduce his new home to easterners. His *Hunting Trips of a Ranchman: Ranch Life and the Hunting Trail,* published in 1885, was a popular introduction to the West. Two years later, he formed the Boone and Crockett Club to advance hunting, exploration, scientific observation, and preservation. His lifelong devotion to the liberating atmosphere of the West would affect his policies when he became influential.

In early October 1886, Roosevelt went back east. At the Republican convention he was nominated for mayor of New York City. He thought it "a hopeless contest," but he wrote that "duty" called. He was pessimistic because his opponents were the rich and upright Abram S. Hewitt on the Democratic ticket and the popular, and seemingly socialist, Henry George on a ticket that asked for a single tax on land, an idea that appealed to poor New Yorkers.

Roosevelt projected himself as the candidate who was oblivious to party politics, class, and color. The time had come for radical reform, he shouted in numerous speeches and visits to various groups of citizens. In an address at Cooper Union, he filled the hall to overflowing. It was a crowd not seen since Lincoln's famous appearance in 1860. Among the hoi polloi were scattered the city's millionaires. Still, all was not going well. Roosevelt described a bleak state of affairs just before the election, in writing to his friend Cabot: "The better element have acted with unscrupulous meanness, and a low, partisan dishonesty, and untruthfulness which would disgrace the veriest machine heelers." His independent Republican friends were about to desert him for Hewitt, the safe Democrat, so strong was their fear of a George victory. Their loyalty to Republicans and to Roosevelt was illusory. Roosevelt came in third. The disappointed cowboy candidate immediately headed back west after thinking, in an idle moment, that he might just stay in his land of "frosted steel." He continued to bounce back and forth across the continent.

The records for the fall of 1886 are sparse, for Roosevelt was carrying the biggest secret of his peregrinating life. He had fallen in love with Edith Carow and planned to marry her; he wanted no publicity. Edith slipped away to London with her family and planned the wedding for December 2. Theodore and Bamie joined her. The two lovers had met again by accident when Roosevelt was visiting his sister in New York. As he came through the door of the house, Edith was coming down the stairs. He wrote to his sister Coni at the time that Edith "was sweet in many different things. . . . I don't think even I had known how wonderfully *good* and unselfish she was; she is naturally reserved and finds it especially hard to express her feelings on paper." In later years he wrote that Edith had made the "real happiness" in his life. It is a tragedy for history that all but two of their intimate letters to each other were burned by Edith. Those she left, however, indicate that Edith and Theodore experienced a full romantic relationship all their years. Their passion for each other never ceased, although he reported that his strong wife "kept him in order."

The new couple took a fifteen-week honeymoon in Europe, and Edith returned pregnant with Theodore Roosevelt, Jr. She insisted that Alice, Roosevelt's daughter by his deceased first wife, join the family, breaking Bamie's heart. She had raised Alice since she was a day old, and she was her family. Bamie did not marry, or have a child, until she was in her forties. Roosevelt now called his daughter Alice and dropped the name Baby Lee. Edith intended to provide Theodore with the warm and tight nuclear family he loved as a youth and she vicariously had shared. In a few years the domestic circle was enlarged with more children, six in all, who provided the great support and comfort of

Edith Kermit Carow Roosevelt

his life. He was a magical and notable father, and his family was more important, he wrote, than any triumph in his several careers.

The Roosevelts settled into Sagamore Hill. His patrimony had dwindled because of his western adventures, which were not profitable, so he threw himself into writing there, something he had always considered a great avocation. *The Naval War of 1812*, which he had started at Harvard when he was twenty-one, was published in 1882. The unemployed husband and father had prospects.

This first book was written with some technical help from his Uncle Bulloch, an experienced navy man of heroic service, and was an instant triumph. A sweeping reconsideration of the navy's role in the war, it was a dramatic retelling and was marked by a rare specificity of detail. Most significant, as it turned out in Roosevelt's future, it implanted the notion of the importance of the navy to a nation's welfare and security. That the naval history corrected the standard anti-American version in English historiography was a mark of its excellence, and English naval historians began to tinker with their own versions of the war. The book remains good reading even today and is available in many editions.

Roosevelt became a prodigious writer in the next few years. Over time he wrote about twenty books, which made him the most literary of all America's presidents. And the writing of these books was in addition to his innumerable articles of opinion and observations. He may have been writing out of necessity, but, as he became skillful, he began to enjoy it a little. He claimed that writing was difficult for him, but his prose shows no evidence of strain. As his family grew and his western ranch drained the family coffers—severe ice storms in the West killed much of his herd of cattle one year—he hunkered down even more to his craft. He would remain a literary man for the rest of his life, no matter what else he was doing. He remarked to Cabot at one point how he was living three parallel lives their friends never knew about. By then he was also civil service commissioner in Washington and the center of a glittering social scene.

Roosevelt wrote at a furious pace. By 1891 he had published eight books, including his studies on ranching, a history of the city of New York, a life of Senator Thomas Hart Benton of Missouri, a biography of the colonial figure Gouverneur Morris of New York, and the first two volumes of his masterpiece, *The Winning of the West*. Several of the early writings deserve some attention because Roosevelt shaped his storytelling around the distinctive American values he thought important, the same values he was making a central part of his own political life. Similarly, his biographies are windows to the person he was writing about as well as to himself. They were a transparent screen to Roosevelt's developing political and social core.

When he was only twenty-eight years old, Roosevelt published his life of Benton, who served fifty years in Washington. Benton was a key western follower of Andrew Jackson. The book shows a rare maturity about the nation's history. It also displays the author's own ripening set of political attitudes. Roosevelt thought the book evolved mainly from his "inner consciousness," so simpatico was he with so many of Benton's political trials. He portrayed Benton as living at a critical juncture, when the federalism of the Founding Fathers had played itself out and a rising Jacksonian democracy was winning elections. He was a transitional figure, bridging the dying political agony of one political regime and the emergence of a new one. In his long life, Benton was unable to weave a seamless web of principles, so Roosevelt called him a follower, not a leader, a representative man of a pioneering people. Though a historian in the making and a still-nascent politician, Roosevelt intuited that a politician must lead the people with an original set of principles, not just mirror those cobbled to the lowest common denominator.

Roosevelt, as yet a moderate expansionist, was sympathetic to Benton's favoring the southern extension of the nation into Texas and westward into Oregon. The author abhorred slavery and its consequences all his life and labeled Benton an anomaly on that issue. Benton didn't much like slavery either, but he was not an abolitionist. Roosevelt, however, took the opportunity to call it an American form of evil and asked for equal justice for the races. He also favored free speech, a burning subject related to slavery. Benton's support of Henry Clay's so-called American System, a collection of bills intended to develop the country with federal money for internal improvements like roads and canals, also won Roosevelt's approval. As he summed up Benton's life, Roosevelt seemed almost to morph into him. He made him into a marble statue, equal in stature only to John Quincy Adams. To Roosevelt, writing about the nation and its people was not a cold, dead retelling of facts but a craft seeking inner truths and morals.

Theodore wrote his biography of Gouverneur Morris, the colonial New Yorker, two years later, at age thirty. Morris he depicted as an admirable figure because of his sound federalist leanings and his able, fearless, and cultivated demeanor. As minister to France during the revolution that ended in the Terror, Morris gained Roosevelt's sympathy by preferring order to upheaval, for Roosevelt was always an enemy of mob violence in his writing and his political life. Ever the nationalist, however, Roosevelt parted with Morris when the latter backed the maritime

New Englanders who wanted to secede from the Union in 1812. President Madison tried to keep America out of the Napoleonic wars and declared an embargo to give neither Britain nor France an opportunity to draw it into a ruinous world conflict. Instead, the embargo ruined New England.

In summing up Morris's life, Roosevelt placed him in the American pantheon along with James Madison, the father of the Constitution; Sam Adams, the supreme revolutionary from Massachusetts; and Patrick Henry of Virginia, whose memorable statement, "Give me liberty or give me death," still rings in schoolchildren's ears today. Roosevelt was too generous.

Roosevelt's masterwork in historical writing was *The Winning of the West*. The first two volumes appeared in 1889 and the latter two in 1894 and 1896. The books were an instant popular and financial success. Roosevelt's goal in tracing the whole movement of peoples from east to west was to tell the tale of individuals and settlers who made a difference in that vast migration. Theodore was interested neither in how the westward movement affected the East nor in how domestic institutions were spread or changed, unlike the brilliant western historian of the day, Frederick Jackson Turner, with whom he was in touch. Rather, Roosevelt concerned himself with the epic and romantic aspects of the West. He wrote of a gifted and robust people who were kin to the fearless sea voyagers of hundreds of years before, who risked their lives to explore the farthest reaches of the globe.

The Winning of the West depicted a relentless battle for land between English-speaking white pioneers and the Indians. When the forests were little more than tangles of woods, the Indians had the edge, and the pioneers, as merciless as their adversaries, fought for every foothold. No quarter was given by either side, and no side was more virtuous than the other, although it was always clear from Roosevelt's telling who would get the prize. Ultimately, Roosevelt was a white man's historian.

All the great pioneers were a large part of the story, from Daniel Boone onward, as well as the great Indian chiefs, such as Logan of the Mingos. The heroism of pioneers, who lived crudely, fought fiercely, and died often cruelly, formed the backbone of the tale. About them Roosevelt wrote, "They were superb individual fighters . . . beautifully drilled in their own discipline, and they were favored beyond measure by the nature of their ground, of which their whole system of warfare enabled them to take the utmost possible benefit." Roosevelt's writing was vivid and immediate, for he had himself lived in the wild and even traced some of the pioneers' paths on horseback. His prose was visceral, relentless.

Of the warfare that conquered Indian tribes, or the "squalid savages" who could not keep the West as "a game preserve," he wrote:

> There are so many dark and bloody pages in the book of border warfare. . . . It contains many a tale of fierce heroism and adventurous ambition, of the daring and resolute courage of men and the patient endurance of women; it shows us a stern race of freemen who toiled hard, endured greatly, and fronted adversity bravely, who prized strength and courage and good faith, whose wives were chaste, who were generous and loyal to their friends. But it shows us also how they spurned at restraint and fretted under it, how they would brook no wrong to them-

selves, and yet too often inflicted wrong on others; their feats of terrible prowess are interspersed with deeds of the foulest and most wanton aggression, the darkest treachery, the most revolting cruelty. . . . We see but little of such qualities as mercy for the fallen, the weak, and the helpless, or pity for a gallant and vanquished foe.

And on the backwoodsmen's families:

Thus the backwoodsmen lived on the clearings they had hewed out of the everlasting forest; a grim, stern people, strong and simple, powerful for good and evil, swayed by gusts of stormy passion, the love of freedom rooted in their very hearts' core. Their lives were harsh and narrow. . . . They were relentless, revengeful, suspicious, knowing neither truth nor pity; they were also upright, resolute, and fearless, loyal to their friends, and devoted to their country.

Roosevelt knew a great set piece when he came upon it, as when he recounted the "finest outburst of savage eloquence" by Logan, a chief of the Mingo tribe, who did not want to make peace in 1774. Rather, Logan described the wrongs inflicted on him and the vengeance he had taken as a warrior:

I appeal to any white man to say if ever he entered Logan's cabin hungry and he gave him not meat; if ever he came cold and naked and he clothed him not? During the course of the last long and bloody war, Logan remained idle in his camp, an advocate for peace. Such was my love for the whites that my countrymen pointed as I passed and said, "Logan is the friend of the white man." I had even thought to have lived with you, but for the injuries of one man. Colonel Cresap the last spring, in cold blood and unprovoked, murdered all the relations of Logan, not even sparing my women and children. There runs not a drop of my blood in the veins of any living creature. This called on me for revenge. I have sought it. I have killed many. I have fully glutted my vengeance. For my country, I rejoice at the beams of peace; but do not harbor a thought that mine is the joy of fear. Logan never felt fear. He will not turn on his heel to save his life. "Who is there to mourn for Logan? Not one."

Logan had misnamed the real murderer of his family, but the frontiersmen who heard or read the speech were very impressed, Roosevelt recounted, despite their hatred of Indians. Logan's speech became a landmark in understanding the first Americans. All the volumes of *The Winning of the West* are still in print today, and they remain among the great classics on the West.

Roosevelt was appointed civil service commissioner in 1889, and he served presidents Benjamin Harrison and Grover Cleveland, Republican and Democrat respectively, "balancing evils" of the parties, as he put it. Tens of thousands of patronage jobs in places like customhouses and post offices were at stake in his post, with implications for corruption.

Against all odds, Roosevelt fought to institute better examinations for appointments and to weed out incompetents and corrupters. He fought off those who spread stories about how unfair his new examinations were by asserting that applicants were being tested only for competence. In a now-famous case, Roosevelt replied to a canard in which an applicant, applying for a job in the post office, was asked how many rings circled the planet Saturn. On looking into the matter, Roosevelt reported that the man was really vying for a post as assistant astronomer in the civil service.

Roosevelt did not think a Republican behaved any better than a Democratic president when it came to patronage—it was rather a choice between the "walrus and the carpenter," he wrote at the time. All presidents knew how important the doling out of loaves and fishes was to the health of a political party. The officeholders provided the infrastructure for the parties. They rounded up votes and contributed a part of their salaries to party coffers. Roosevelt estimated that his greatest victory was that he put twenty-five thousand more persons under civil service—there were tens of thousands of patronage jobs—nearly doubling the number previously on the merit system. He also improved the administration of the civil service law. He claimed that he rooted out some of the most corrupt officials, and he did indeed fight some great and successful battles. The record shows that, almost always, he fought for better appointments for people than those being suggested by politicians or party influentials, whether for significant or lowly posts. Roosevelt's six years as commissioner gave him an apprenticeship in running a large, quasi-political bureaucracy. It was a step up in his career.

As notably successful as Roosevelt's commissioner's job was his social life. Theodore and Edith's years in Washington were happy ones. He found Washington to be a graspable prize and viewed the city as a pleasant village. He took a neighborhood view of Washington, one built on social relations. It was the foreigners who dwelled on architecture and design. They openly admired the capital's clean and dazzlingly white appearance, with its imposing marble buildings and broad avenues shaded by tens of thousands of trees. They called it a new Rome.

The more prosaic Roosevelt plunged right in to his new social environment, entertaining as though he were still in a smaller world. In Washington, social life depended on officeholders who had money beyond their salaries and who could, therefore, entertain lavishly in sumptuous houses. These leading lights mixed business with pleasure all the time, something Roosevelt found new but bracing. That the Roosevelts lived in modest circumstances was irrelevant; he fit into the Washington social scene because he came from an elite background and held an important position.

At first, the unexpectedly frugal Roosevelt settled his family in a small house at 1820 Jefferson Place NW, where they scarcely had room. He later moved everyone to a larger home at 1215 Nineteenth Street NW. Both places are still standing, although neither is a family house. Unabashed by their middle-class circumstances, the Roosevelts entertained guests about twice a week and were invited out to dinner on three or four nights. Their closest friends remained Bostonians, although others were added to the Roosevelt circle, including diplomats, politicians, scientists, and men of letters. The Roosevelts' intimate social circle included Senator Henry Cabot Lodge of Massachusetts and his handsome wife, Nanny. Cabot was to become Theodore's best friend, although the senator was ten years older. Then there were rich couples like the Bellamy Storers of Ohio, who were champions of Catholic matters; the Winthrop Chanlers and the Henry Adamses (he was the grandson and great-grandson of presidents) from his early days; and Cecil Spring Rice, an Englishman who had been best man at the Roosevelts' secret wedding in London—they had met on the ship en route—and who became ambassador to the United States a few years later.

Also in the Roosevelts' circle were Senator James Donald Cameron of Pennsylvania and his wife, Elizabeth, a stunning redhead given the palm as the most beautiful woman in the city. When Adams became a widower, she was his secret, and unrequited, love. Always about were John Hay and his wife. The gentle and knowing Hay would always be close to Roosevelt. Hay would become Nanny Lodge's lover in 1890, but we do not know if the puritanical Roosevelt ever knew. Hay had been one of Lincoln's secretaries, and he was then writing what would be a multivolume and magisterial biography of the Civil War president, Roosevelt's greatest political hero and the touchstone for his political life. Most of Roosevelt's intimates would be with him again when he was president, for, as President John F. Kennedy would say, the presidency is not a good place to make friends.

Roosevelt always admired writers and adventurers, and he recorded his impressions of some of the memorable ones who dined at his table. He described Rudyard Kipling as a pleasant little man, bright, nervous, voluble, but rather underbred. Then there was the anthropologist Frank Hamilton Cushing, who had discovered the Seven Cities of Cibola and spent six years with the Zunis in New Mexico, learning the nature of the Indian secret societies.

Gregarious to a fault, Roosevelt was on the go day and night, working and spending time with his family and friends, riding and hiking. It sometimes seemed to his visitors that they had to have a horse, or hiking gear, to keep up with the commissioner, for he preferred to be in motion while being visited. He noted that he ate and drank too much wine at dinners, for he enjoyed them so much. He described himself as looking like a walrus, weighing two hundred pounds and standing five feet eight. But he could not curb his irrepressible self and curtail his overflowing schedule of social events. He recorded that he had a "Macawber-like," or cavalier temperament regarding finances, for his standard of living put him twenty-five hundred dollars in debt after six years as commissioner—a hefty sum of money, probably more than fifty thousand dollars today.

The commissioner had a vital radiance and was irresistible as a companion. Theodore was open and friendly, a natty dresser in gray trousers and a boy's wide-brimmed hat. He remained totally self-assured. The acerbic Henry Adams described him as pure act, something like a medieval and indescribable force. He also recorded that Roosevelt was a new kind of creature, only recently discovered—one that radiates warmth and attracts men as the sun attracts lizards.

Then, in 1895, Roosevelt and his family left Washington. He had been appointed a police commissioner of New York City and was quickly chosen by the other members of the commission to be its president. The returning New Yorker had become an imposing figure—thick-necked with a large, muscled chest. His face was permanently tanned from ranch life; he wore his abundant hair short, had a high, almost hoarse voice; and he dressed in high style. His eyeglasses might belie his strength at a challenger's peril. He

HE'S ALL RIGHT WHEN YOU KNOW HIM· BUT YOU'VE GOT TO KNOW HIM FIRST."
[From Yesterday's Evening Telegram.]

Cartoon of Theodore Roosevelt as
New York Police Commissioner, 1895

was not to be trifled with, except by cartoonists, who never had a better time plying their trade. They loved depicting Roosevelt with a mouth full of enormous white teeth. More often than not, that mouth was emitting colorful, memorable statements. Cartoonists exaggerated his growing girth, his gold-topped cane, and his idiosyncratic cape. The worst lampooning occurred in later years, when the satirists also encased lively statements in their balloons. When he was top policeman, cartoonists were just getting started. One called him Teddy the Scorcher, as he was cleaning up the city. Another put him in an old Dutch outfit lighting a lamp on a corner and awakening startled policemen. This caricature was called "THE SEQUEL—The Dutch Patriot Catches 'Em Napping."

Roosevelt was completely absorbed in his new job, arriving at work at nine in the morning and not leaving until six or even eight in the evening. He lived in the city during the week, having rented Bamie's house on Madison Avenue. In warm weather he traveled to Sagamore Hill, where his family resided and the children attended the local public school. He commuted from there to work on the train. For exercise he rode to the station on a bicycle, which had just been invented. (Roosevelt loved new inventions, becoming the first president to travel in a submarine and on an airplane.) Still, he was getting flabby from too much desk work and not enough activity. His time riding, chopping wood, and canoeing was limited to weekends. Nevertheless, he was still in good, if not great, shape.

Theodore's love for his job sustained him. His signature police activity was the night walk. He wore a black cape and wielded a cane and prowled the city accompanied by newspaper reporters, looking for misbehaving policemen. These strolls kept him awake a marathon forty hours, but he had endured such strains before as a ranch hand on a roundup. Roosevelt uncovered policemen sleeping, imbibing in watering holes, and frequenting brothels while on duty. The reporters got sensational stories, and the commissioner got much-needed publicity for his campaign to reform the police. Roosevelt became the superstar of his time because of the stories and articles written about his seemingly bizarre activities. Up until this time, his several jobs had not allowed for the possibility of becoming famous. But now that he was a crime buster in the nation's largest and richest city became news, and the reform-minded and the middle class could not get enough of him.

The commissioner's walks during the day, almost as famous as his night walks, gave him an opportunity to see for the first time the city's numerous and various citizens, so unlike the delicate begonias of his own class. Once more he visited tenements, this time under the tutelage of reformers like Jacob Riis, the famous investigative journalist and photographer who had shaken the conscience of New Yorkers such as Roosevelt with his portrayal of the city's slums in *Scribner's Magazine* and with his book, *How the Other Half Lives,* which Roosevelt had read. Then, through Riis and other reporters like him, Roosevelt came to know Samuel Gompers, the leader of the new labor movement. Once, working men had been sturdy members of the middle class; now they had been reduced almost to a status like that of the slave.

Observing firsthand and collecting facts, as his scientific training had taught him, Roosevelt was appalled by what he saw. He made several visits to the slums, twice on his own, and wrote down his findings:

> There were one, two, or three room apartments, and the work of manufacturing the tobacco by men, women, and children, went on day and night in the eating, living, and sleeping rooms—sometimes in one room. . . . The tobacco was stowed about everywhere, alongside the foul bedding, and in a corner where there were scraps of food.

Roosevelt knew that something had to be done, and he took action. As police president he closed down hundreds of tenements for incredible violations of the city's health regulations. He aimed to improve housing and health conditions, and not only for the unfortunate tobacco workers. He strove to make factories safer and demanded the enforcement of labor regulations already on the books. Administrative action could get things done when the lawmaking body—in this case, the state legislature—was uninterested. This time it helped the laboring man. Roosevelt would find other uses for this tool for other causes later in his political life.

Publicity was the fuel of Roosevelt's engine of reform. After evil was exposed it would end, he believed. Meantime, his political career "rose like a rocket," as he described it. Roosevelt's mastery of public relations played a significant role in his ascent. He thought that if he could not get the dominant role in the Republican Party, he would force the issue by becoming popular. Popularity won elections.

As police commissioner, Roosevelt was forced to confront graft to an extraordinary degree. Jobs in the department were fought over because patrolmen earned fourteen hundred dollars a year, with sergeants and other officers being paid as much as six thousand, significantly more than the average middle-class income at that time. Of course, few would admit to the monies policemen collected from graft and crime, but it became known during one investigation by a New York state commission how utterly wealthy top police officials had become. One chief of police admitted to the investigators that he was worth the enormous sum of $350,000. (Roosevelt fired him.)

Not only did legal and illegal businesses pay off the police (tens of thousands of dollars exchanged hands), but the police jobs themselves were available for a price. The de-

partment had the incredible number of thirty-eight thousand positions, and they often were sold for three hundred
to fifteen thousand dollars. Even these prices were not
onerous, for dishonest policemen could earn it back, and
much more, by shaking down businesses. Policemen, it was
known, contributed a percentage of their pay and loot to
party officials. It was an orderly business, police corruption. Of the $15 million police budget, two-thirds came
from corruption. It was this kind of political system, controlled mostly by Tammany Hall, as the Democratic
Party's office was known, that men like Roosevelt and
other reformers had excoriated over the years.

To reform the system Roosevelt introduced new examinations for policemen. As a result, sixteen hundred qualified men were given jobs as officers. Within two years,
about two-fifths of all patrolmen were placed under the
revamped civil service, or about four times the previous
number of protected jobholders. The qualifying examinations were not onerous. An applicant had to know how to
spell, to write a good letter, to do basic arithmetic, and
to have some acquaintance with history and geography.
To those complaining about the unfairness of the test,
Roosevelt made public several examples of failing replies
that would-be patrolmen had offered. In answer to the
question "What are the five New England states?" a man
wrote, "Ireland, Scotland, Whales, and Cork." Another
applicant who failed wrote the word *paper* in answer to
"Upon what instrument is the government of the United
States founded?" One applicant hoped to flatter Roosevelt by replying "President Roosevelt" when asked who
would perform the duties of the mayor if he were absent
or disabled.

Just as importantly, Roosevelt made appointments regardless of color, creed, religion, or politics. When challenged about appointing blacks, he openly defended his policy. The blacks were qualified. As a Republican whose ideal was Abraham Lincoln, Roosevelt would always be color-blind and guided by the tenet of equality. It was usually Democrats who complained—his correspondence shows this—about this application of equality as a principle, but the Commissioner held firm then and later, when he held other government positions.

At the time, the police were part of the election system. They oversaw the registration of voters, the printing of ballots (each party had its own), and the actual voting. For decades, the police helped their party or looked the other way at ballot stuffing. By implementing a hiring system that took no account of political affiliation, Roosevelt was instrumental in the first clean election in the city's history in 1896.

However, he made one very costly mistake as police commissioner during his two-year term, which was politically damaging, when he decided to uphold a new excise law that closed saloons on Sunday. He always claimed that his job was to enforce the law. And he knew that this particular enforcement would upend the unspoken social contract Republicans had with their only significant immigrant group, the German Americans, but he was bullheaded. One can only speculate whether he abhorred liquor because it was destroying the life of Elliott, his beloved brother. Elliott had become a public drunkard and had a mistress, having abandoned his wife and children, his little girl being Eleanor Roosevelt.

There were more than twelve thousand saloons in the city, and the proprietors of each and every one wanted to be open on Sunday, when working men took their recreation. Most workers toiled fifty-seven hours in a six-day week, and they went to saloons, often with their families, to relax and to catch up on politics, for the saloon was also a political clubhouse. Roosevelt put an end to this, enraging a whole class of working men. The Irish had been voting Democratic, and the German Americans had favored the Republicans. This would change. Roosevelt also quietly angered many policemen, who did not like arresting their social equals for the seemingly harmless crime of tippling on Sunday. One anonymous person was so enraged by the reform that he sent Roosevelt a bomb in the mail.

Roosevelt fought an intense battle, but he scored only a pyrrhic victory. At the next general election, German Americans made a revolutionary political switch to the Democrats. One estimate was that thirty thousand German Americans left their longtime home in the Republican Party, in which they practically elected Lincoln twice, as they provided the margins for victory in some states. Republican leaders were aghast, and the Democrats took the city in the next election. The cacophony was so great, and Republican leaders were so stunned by Roosevelt's blunder, that they began to consider passing a law to clip a police commissioner's powers in New York City.

Roosevelt thought that he might be legislated out of office. As a precaution against being unemployed, he cast an eye elsewhere for a position. He would always need a job to support his growing family and his lifestyle. Moreover, he did not want his children to see him idle. He asked his friends, like Cabot, whether they could secure him the job of assistant secretary of the navy, which he thought would admirably suit his talents. His fantasies of heroic military deeds when he was a lad, his Confederate uncle's valiant role in the Civil War, and his history of the navy in the War of 1812 all pointed in that direction. Most important, he had never left the Republican Party despite his disagreements with it, nor had he bolted after Blaine was nominated in 1884, as did scores of independent, or other reforming Republicans.

Roosevelt asked that his friends disabuse the new Republican president, William McKinley, of the idea that he was too rambunctious and was not a loyal party man. He would follow McKinley's lead, even his nonreformist political tendencies. The confident Roosevelt, bursting with ambition, who had a taste for power in Albany, Washington, and New York City, now wanted a high-profile job of national significance. He was taking a keen interest in international affairs and was attuned to what was happening beyond the oceans protecting the country. The rise of new and aggressive nation states and their scramble for imperial domains in Africa, Latin America, and Asia concerned him. How would the nation defend itself in such a dangerous world? It would be the navy's job, but that military organization and its ships had to at least be equal to the sailors and modern ships of these rising countries. Roosevelt would leave behind domestic politics, where he had had some successes but suffered plenty of bruises, and step onto the world stage.

From McKinley's side, the message was that he wanted a peaceful administration. He had had enough strife as an officer in the Civil War. He was going to be content to allow the Congress to lead and the leaders of the party to tell the Congress what to do. It would be the standard Republican mode of operating since after Lincoln's day. Roosevelt's friends signaled to the new president that the tyro from New York understood what was expected. He would be a leashed lion.

CHAPTER 4

The Arc of Power

As regards Hawaii . . . if I had my way we would annex those islands tomorrow. If that is impossible I would establish a protectorate over them. I believe we should build a Nicaraguan canal at once, and in the meantime that we should build a dozen new battleships, half of them on the Pacific Coast. . . . I am fully alive to the danger from Japan. . . . We should acquire the Danish Islands [later called the Virgin Islands, when acquired by the US], and by turning Spain out should serve notice that no strong European power, and especially not Germany, should be allowed to gain a foothold.

———

I was not acting in accordance with orders. I had been told to *support* the attack of the regulars with my regiment. I moved through the 9th Regiment, of my own accord and gave the order to charge, and led in person that portion of the line on horseback, being the first man on the Hill, and killing a Spaniard with my own hands. I led in person the next charge on the second line of block-houses. I led in person the third charge; and then at the extreme front commanded the fragments of the six cavalry regiments and brigade until the next morning.

———

Memory plays funny tricks in such a fight, where things happen quickly, and all kinds of mental images succeed one another in a detached kind of way, while the work goes on. As I gave the order in question [to rush the entrenchments of the Spanish on San Juan hill] there slipped through my mind Mahan's account of Nelson's orders that each ship as it sailed forward, if it saw another ship engaged with an enemy's ship, should rake the latter as it passed. . . . [I] ordered a charge on my own hook.

BY THE END OF THE 1890s, THEODORE Roosevelt was on an ascending arc of power and responsibility. On April 19, 1897, President McKinley appointed him assistant secretary of the navy, a post he would find more challenging than his previous stint as civil service commissioner. Once more, he gobbled up myriad details of his job—planning, organizing, and setting operational policy—often breaking old boundaries. Roosevelt provided robust leadership to make the navy the stronger of the two military arms of the nation.

When Roosevelt took up the post, he needed no introduction to the theory and practice of naval operations and to international relations. It seemed that all his life he had been interested in the sea and its consequences for the nation bounded by two vast oceans, with friendly Canada to the north and Mexico to the south. The hero tales told by his Aunt Anna about his Uncle James Bulloch about the Confederate navy had mesmerized the

Theodore Roosevelt as Assistant Secretary of the Navy, 1898

little boy. Then young Theodore's naval history of the War
of 1812 rekindled his seafaring interest. As an adult, Roosevelt's keen interest in the doings of the rising imperial
powers of Europe gave him a sophisticated worldview. His
cosmopolitanism led him to favor a large, strong navy

with new, heavy vessels and the latest technology; the re-assertion of the Monroe Doctrine, that is, of keeping foreign governments out of the affairs of the Americas; a forward position in the Pacific to protect the West Coast; and a recognition by the superpowers of Europe that the United States would protect its national interests.

The Rooseveltian view of the nation's destiny could be seen as the necessity to expand west and south behind a powerful navy; as imperialism, the old term for conquering foreign and less-developed peoples; or as jingoism, a new term then of derision for those bursting for war. Yet, the secretary's plunge into world affairs as a large player was irresistible. It can be argued that as any nation industrialized and made more products than it could consume and as it grew bumper crops, looking outward became as natural as the beat of rain. The spirit of the age was expressed in just this joining of immense material wealth with a rambunctious American nature.

Roosevelt thought that most Americans were not ready for the role he believed the new age demanded. At first, he cast a somewhat cold eye on many of his fellow Americans, except for those in the armed services and their engineers, the police who kept order, and other hard-working toilers. He compared Americans with the Slavs [Russians], the English, and the French, who were also experiencing the rough and tumble of materialism and expansionism. Roosevelt saw some hope, however, for his fellow countrymen, if the "rude strength" of the founding age could be put behind a high national purpose. In 1887, in a private letter, he voiced these both unkind and hopeful views about the American condition:

We are barbarians of a certain kind, and what is most unpleas-ant we are barbarians with a certain middle-class, Philistine quality of ugliness and pettiness, raw conceit, and raw sensi-tiveness. Where we get highly civilized, as in the northeast, we seem to become civilized in an unoriginal and ineffective way, and tend to die out. . . . The commercial and cheap altruistic spirit . . . the spirit of the banker, the broker, the mere manufac-turer, and mere merchant, is unpleasantly prominent. I cannot see that we have lost vigor compared to what we were a century ago. If anything I think we have gained it. In political matters we are often very dull mentally, and especially morally; but even in political matters there is plenty of rude strength, and I don't think we are as badly off as we were in the days of Jeffer-son, for instance. We are certainly better off as we were in the days of Buchanan.

Roosevelt set his course to inspire and lead an American national political revival, and he never wavered or looked back.

Roosevelt reveled in his work with the navy. While Sec-retary of the Navy John Davis Long took a full summer va-cation in 1897, Roosevelt took over, as was the practice, as acting secretary; that is, he was in full charge of affairs. In his day-to-day work as naval assistant secretary, he was in charge of several bureaus: engineering for steam, the sci-ences of hydrology and astronomy, naval law, diplomacy, fi-nance, strategy, and education. And there were the tasks of relating to Congress, to the president, and to the press.

Roosevelt also undertook the arduous task of looking after promotions. He did not favor promoting officers on the basis of seniority or on political recommendations, to the horror of some old navy men and politicians. He promoted officers on the basis of merit, however outrageous that seemed. He also gave equal rank to the newly skilled engineers and to line officers, as electricity was put into renovated ships. There is no evidence that the vacationing Secretary Long was interested in such changes, which Roosevelt studiously reported to him in long letters, but he did not object. Then, too, Roosevelt left the sweltering heat in Washington to inspect various dry docks and ships; as he put it while on the seas, he "gyrated" around the fleet. He always had to see for himself what was going on. He was never a desk jockey.

Roosevelt's informal activities, however, proved almost as significant as his assigned duties. He became part of an informal brains trust on naval power and imperial issues. Comprising a small circle of Washington clubmen, the group was informed by the highly influential strategist and his new mentor, Captain Alfred T. Mahan. A former naval officer during the Civil War, Mahan had later served two stints as president of the Naval War College. But he was perhaps best known for his controversial books, *The Influence of Sea Power upon History, 1660–1783* (1890) and *The Influence of Sea Power upon the French Revolution and Empire, 1793–1812* (1892), in which he showed that naval power had played the determining role in European conflicts and the wars between France and England. Mahan's argument that the navy was more essential to America's interest than the army seemed radical in a nation dependent on fixed fortifications and boots on the ground. But Roosevelt took to Mahan's ideas instinctively. He wrote "personal and private" letters to Mahan to give his thoughts—not the government's—and to "sympathize" with Mahan's views. Only to his old friend Cabot was he this open.

Roosevelt was not rethinking the navy in a vacuum. He always wanted to see the big picture, and the immediate world scene provided the background for his planning: Hawaii was in political turmoil, and he feared that Japan might try to grab it. The United States ought to annex it quickly, he thought. A canal ought to be built through Nicaragua so that warships could move from ocean to ocean swiftly, as there were not enough ships to put on permanent station in the many areas where they were needed—in the Atlantic, the Pacific, Europe, the Mediterranean, and the Caribbean. Roosevelt's broad vision of naval power went beyond most Americans' dreams, but it was a realistic response to the instability beginning to trouble the world.

At the time, the United States had only a one-ocean navy in terms of size, and it was scattered. Compared with European navies, it was probably fifth in combat power, England's being first. Roosevelt was especially wary of Spain, which owned Cuba and had possessions in the Pacific as well, the Philippines and Samoa. Ninety miles off Florida, Cuba had been a hotbed of insurrection for a decade. Roosevelt's master idea, stated in private letters, was that the United States ought to own all the islands near its mainland, Cuba and Hawaii chief among them. He thought that President McKinley ought to take the initiative with Spain concerning Cuba and not just react to its genocidal acts against insurgents and even innocents. The Spanish army was ruthless toward revolutionaries, and it set up concentration camps where they held two hundred thousand women and children virtually to die from lack of care. In November 1897, in a private letter, Roosevelt wrote:

> I would regard a war with Spain from two standpoints: first the advisability on the grounds both of humanity and self interest of interfering on behalf of the Cubans, and of taking one more step toward the complete freeing of America from European dominion; second the benefit done our people by giving them something to think of which isn't material gain, and especially the benefit done our military forces by trying both the Navy and Army in actual practice. . . . I believe that war will have to, or at least ought to, come sooner or later; and I think we should prepare for it well in advance.

Roosevelt was a veritable dynamo in figuring out what the navy needed to support his ambitions for the country. By the end of September, in his first year as assistant secretary, he made his recommendations to Secretary Long. He requested six new battleships, six large cruisers, and seventy-five torpedo boats. New dry docks should be built, he wrote, and he recommended heavier armor, larger guns, and smokeless powder for all new ships and for refitted older ships.

But once again, Roosevelt found himself blocked by politics. Within weeks he learned that he would get only one new battleship and a few torpedo boats. Once more, but now in the large national arena, he was out of step with his fellow Republicans, who were conservative and penny-pinching. And he had no other allies. The Democrats were not supporting any great expenses for naval expansion or a muscular foreign policy. Despite the obstacles, Roosevelt never let up trying to build up the navy. In private letters he started calling himself a "jingo," a belligerent, in foreign affairs.

Then, on February 15, 1898, Roosevelt was handed an opportunity when the American battleship *Maine* was blown up in Havana harbor. Packed with explosives, the ship was a floating bomb. Two hundred sixty-two of the sailors aboard were killed instantly or died later of wounds. From the outset, Roosevelt doubted that anyone would ever be able to determine whether the explosion was an accident or the result of sabotage by Spain. (He was right; to this day the cause of the explosion remains undetermined.) Later, Roosevelt railed against Spain privately, coming close to accusing it of sabotage, but he spent more time using the disaster to fulfill his own military plans. He immediately asked for a second new battleship to make up for the *Maine* and gave a plan to Secretary Long for a redeployment of all navy ships to not only protect them but also to put them in positions to defend the country against Spain. While crafting his strategic plan, however, he worried about the six-to-eight ratio of American big ships to those of Spain.

At the White House, President McKinley was bent on keeping the peace. He saw no clouds on the horizon but was not opposed to Roosevelt's naval buildup. Congress, however, was, so little was done beyond Roosevelt's recommendations for more naval training, better pay for navy men who had been reorganized in their tasks, and more electricity to make ships more efficient.

THE ACTIVIST in the navy department probably would have been even more energetic but for the distractions in his family. Edith was seriously ill after giving birth to her fifth child and Roosevelt's sixth. At first she suffered from a prolonged and worrying grippe, but as time went by it became clear that she was failing from some other cause. Roosevelt watched her hover between life and death. Fearful that he would lose another wife, he took the time to get the best medical advice from The Johns Hopkins Hospital's world-renowned Dr. William Osler. He found that Edith had an abscess on the hip which needed immediate and dangerous surgery. At the same time, Ted Jr. and Kermit also became ill. Ted was having blinding headaches; Kermit's ailment was never disclosed. A harried Roosevelt tried to cope with his family's prolonged sicknesses. As one friend noted, he was always coolest when under pressure, even when under fire. As the months passed and the Roosevelts mended, the husband and father regained his zest.

Of all the hot spots needing his attention, Roosevelt fixed on the long insurrection in Cuba. In his view, Spain was a colonial power still living in the medieval world of the infamous General Alva and the bestial priest Torquemada. Meanwhile, the "yellow" press, as Roosevelt called it (the precursor of the modern tabloid), was screaming for war. Newspaper editors knew that the hysteria would send circulation skyrocketing; indeed, they sold from one to five million copies of these papers daily on the basis of incendiary headlines and stories. Almost inevitably, given the emotional state of the nation, Congress stepped into action, passing a bill authorizing fifty million dollars for the construction of three battleships, sixteen destroyers, fourteen torpedo boats, four submarines, and funds to buy auxiliary ships abroad.

Roosevelt was elated, if puzzled, by the sudden activity after so much delay and palaver. Knowing that even with this increased funding, little could be done in time to prepare for an imminent war with new ships and equipment, he was delegated to purchase auxiliary ships for conversion into warships. Roosevelt pounced. His days of fuming privately while rowing his war boat with muffled oars were over.

Despite great effort, however, Roosevelt was not able to accumulate an especially impressive flotilla. He sourly wrote to a friend that he had secured only one unarmed cruiser, two second-rate torpedo boats, and twelve tugs, yachts, and merchant steamers. It was hardly enough to push Spain out of the Western Hemisphere, but Roosevelt knew that the main theater of war against Spain would be on land in Cuba. Most of the nation's fleet was in the Pacific, and it was a formidable force under the command of the redoubtable Admiral George Dewey. It would provide the essential naval action if called upon. Its immediate mission was to prevent Spain from defending the Philippines, its major colony in the Pacific, but the fleet could steam where it was needed. Never far from Roosevelt's mind was embattled and undefended Hawaii.

President McKinley finally sent in his war message on April 19, exactly a year after Roosevelt had taken office. This difficult decision by the pacific McKinley followed the report in late March by the court of inquiry on the sinking of the *Maine,* in which the cause of the explosion was deemed uncertain and blame was placed on an external device (thus absolving Spain and the U.S. Navy, the latter of possible incompetence). In addition, proposals from McKinley to Spain to negotiate differences had been rebuffed. Exasperated, the president had sent an ultimatum that included an armistice, which the proud Spaniards rejected. By early April, McKinley began writing his war message.

Congress responded to the president by declaring war on Spain on April 24. The navy, unlike the army, was in very good shape for a conflict, thanks to Roosevelt. It was well trained and efficient, had supplies on hand and good guns on ships, and was located in strategic places.

Although the army was a sluggish military force compared with the navy, Roosevelt, sensing where events were taking the nation, began angling for an army appointment some weeks before war was declared. Unlike his father, who had avoided serving in the Civil War, Roosevelt itched to get into the fight. He had served three years in New York's national guard and, in letters he wrote to those in charge of New York's militia, claimed that he knew how to command men. He had no martial experience on the sea and never thought of serving in the navy he had so painstakingly rebuilt. The day after the declaration of war, Roosevelt received his appointment in the army. The president called for 125,000 men to be added to the 28,000 serving, and he added three regiments of frontiersmen who were used to rifles and horses. Roosevelt was offered the command of the first of these. He demurred and preferred, wisely, to be second in command of the First Voluntary Cavalry under Colonel Leonard Wood.

Roosevelt was satisfied that he had done all he could to prepare the navy for war and to position it for action. His last naval order, delivered via cablegram on February 25, 1898, was:

=========== **CABLEGRAM** ===========

Dewey, Hong Kong—Order the squadron, except the *Monocracy* to Hong Kong. Keep full of coal. In the event of declaration of war [against] Spain, our duty will be to see that the Spanish squadron does not leave the Asiatic coast, and then offensive operations in Philippines. Keep *Olympia* until further orders.

At that time, Secretary Long wrote in his diary that Roosevelt "has gone at things like a bull in a china shop." Publicly, however, he said nothing. The records show that Roosevelt had spent at least ten months of feverish work building the new navy and had written numerous full letters to Long on the strengthening of the force and its necessary disposition in the world. As well, he wrote brilliant letters to the secretary laying out naval strategies to protect the nation and to win a war against Spain, if it came. From time to time, Roosevelt also met with the president, with whom he had cordial relations, to brief him on naval affairs and strategy.

Roosevelt's family was still not fully well. Edith was now healthy, but young Ted was suffering from a nervous breakdown and was sent to live with his Aunt Corinne in Connecticut. In a private letter his father wrote that he thought he had pushed his son too hard. Undeterred by his family troubles, however, Roosevelt continued his preparations to join his regiment. He reorganized his finances, sold his cattle, gave up his ranch, and took out a life insurance policy. He calculated that his family no longer needed his financial support, even if he died.

Gone for a soldier, Roosevelt had recruited a regiment of 1,000 men, although only 565 actually went to Cuba. Roosevelt described his force as three-quarters cowboys and stockmen. Ninety-five percent of the men were native born, including a score of Indians, a score of Mexicans, fifty southerners, and fifty easterners from the best colleges and clubs. The easterners included well-known tennis players, a master of hounds, and a top steeplechase rider. Among the westerners were a sheriff, a marshall, and two Crocketts. He calculated that two-thirds of his men had fathers who fought in the Civil War, always remembering that his own father had not. The men were mostly property holders, and, as was the custom, they elected their own junior officers.

The multimillionaire officer John Jacob Astor gave Roosevelt's regiment the munificent gift of a fully equipped battery—worth about a hundred thousand dollars at the time and millions today. The men wore brown uniforms to distinguish them from the regular army, which dressed in blue. The eastern swells sported Abercrombie & Fitch shirts and custom-crafted boots. Some preferred flared British breeches. Roosevelt wore a khaki uniform with bright yellow trim that he had ordered from Brooks Brothers. Each man was issued a Colt revolver and a Krag-Jorgenson magazine carbine (no single-shot Springfields for them!). Only officers were allowed to have horses on the crowded ships, so the Rough Riders soon became rough walkers.

Roosevelt was on the high seas on June 14, after impatiently waiting for six days on a crowded ship in Tampa harbor. The delay was caused by the "mismanagement" of the army, he reported to Cabot. Still, the colonel had the best-equipped and best-trained regiment in the army. His spirits returned, and he mused that his men could whip Caesar's legendary Tenth Legion. He even became positively romantic in his letters. He wrote to his sister Corinne:

> Today we are steaming southward through a sapphire sea, wind-rippled, under an almost cloudless sky. There are some forty-eight craft in all, in three columns, the black hulls of the transports setting off the gray hulls of the men-of-war. Last evening we stood up on the bridge and watched the red sun sink and the lights blaze up on the ships, for miles ahead and astern, while the band played piece after piece, from the "Star Spangled Banner" . . . to "The Girl I Left Behind Me." But it is a great historical expedition, and I thrill to feel that I am a part of it.

The 133 days that Roosevelt spent in Cuba were a rollercoaster ride for the inexperienced soldier whose only training was in the unserious New York militia. He began recording his experiences in a remarkable series of letters to Cabot. At one extreme, Roosevelt wrote, he witnessed the almost total mismanagement of the administrative, business, and mechanical workings of the army and, at the other, the incredible bravery of the fighting men. Roosevelt thought the top army leadership remote, the supplies of food, clothing, and material badly distributed and even lacking at times, and the military tactics sometimes improvisational. Slightly more than fifteen thousand men were sent to Cuba with just over eight hundred officers. Something like four hundred men were added as auxiliaries. About twenty-three hundred horses and mules went along. Firepower included gatling guns, mortars, howitzers, a cannon, and siege and light guns.

The master strategy for the Cuban venture called for the taking of the port of Santiago, the capital, not with a frontal assault but from the rear, by land. That would lead to the collapse of the Spanish army. As the American armada neared Cuban shores in June 1898, the army and navy commanders went ashore to meet General Calixto Garcia, the leader of the Cuban insurrectionists. He was gigantic, with a wound on his forehead that was even more impressive than his erect stance and snow-white mustache extending beyond the sides of his face. Together they planned the immediate landing of six or seven thousand troops of the Fifth Corps in a small, almost-deserted village with the quaint name of Daquiri, eighteen miles east of Santiago. Seven miles west of this site, another force of about the same size was to disembark at the port of Siboney, where the Fifth Corps was to march to meet them. Using the main road, the forces were to engage in a joint operation toward the prize of Santiago.

On June 22, guns from the ships were fired into the ramshackle first village, already set on fire by the fleeing Spaniards. From "truck-cars" on the ships, bands played tunes, the favorite being "There'll Be a Hot Time in the Old Town Tonight." The Rough Riders disembarked ahead of schedule, with the assistance of an old navy friend of Roosevelt's who had maneuvered his ship to favor them. The men leaped onto slick and rotting docks in heavy surf like skilled jumping horses, while Roosevelt oversaw the lifting of his two horses. Losing one mount in the water brought him to swear like the trooper he was becoming.

Theodore Roosevelt with the Rough Riders at San Juan, Cuba, 1898

Under their aggressive colonel the Rough Riders were the first cavalry forces ashore. The nearsighted Roosevelt, who had twelve pairs of eyeglasses sewed into his hat and other places, was on Cuban soil, spoiling for a fight. Neither he nor anyone else saw any Spaniards, and not a shot was fired to impede the landing. The American troops yelled, "*Viva* Cuba *libre*." Their Cuban rebel allies replied, "*Viva los* Americanos." The Rough Riders ran up the first American flag over Cuba, and the band played "The Star-Spangled Banner." It was a picture-perfect beginning to what would become a bloody battle for Cuban freedom and, in Roosevelt's view, American manhood. For the Spanish, it was the beginning of the end of their 382-year rule over Cuba, the jewel of its western empire.

The first battle, for Las Guasimas, named after the pass about twelve miles from Santiago, was fought against entrenched Spaniards on high ground. It was short and bloody. On June 23, two columns of regular soldiers deployed from Siboney to Santiago were to meet at an all-important pass in the terrain marked by the body of a dead guerrilla. One column of blues was to be commanded by General S. B. M. Young, a former general in the Union army. Another was to be led by a former general of the Confederates, the irrepressible "Fighting Joe" Wheeler. Wheeler wished to go to the meeting point first, beating the other column, which he viewed as an enemy Yankee adversary. Roosevelt's Rough Riders formed a separate, parallel column.

The Rough Riders slogged their way toward Las Guasimas through the terrible heat of the jungle and the dense underbrush. Along the way, Roosevelt heard strange noises mimicking cuckoos and wood doves. At one point he noticed cut barbed wire, as a good cowboy would. But he did not understand that the birdcalls he heard were actually lookout noises, and he did not connect the cut wire to the passage of Spaniards toward the nearby high ridge. Nor did anyone else. Soon enough, Spanish sharpshooters aimed a fierce barrage at the soldiers from on high, using modern Mauser rifles and smokeless powder to hide their exact whereabouts.

The first casualty of war was the Adonis-like Rough Rider Hamilton Fish, Roosevelt's young friend, a member of New York's elite, and the son of a former U.S. senator and cabinet member under President Ulysses S. Grant. Then a second friend fell and several more men were cut down in the fusillade. Thirty-four men were wounded while Roosevelt, staying on his feet during the carnage, miraculously was not hit.

Roosevelt was soon ordered to take three troops of men into the thickets to face the Spanish who were shooting from the high ground. The Rough Riders put down such shattering volleys of fire that the Spanish scurried away from the topmost point on the ridge, exposing themselves to crossfire from the Rough Riders and the army regulars.

The path was now open for the American lines to advance along the front, with Roosevelt leading the extreme left flank. About nine hundred men in all—Roosevelt with more than half of the forces—ran out into the open, rushing between fifteen hundred and two thousand Spaniards. At one point, Roosevelt led the charge with a wounded man's rifle, his sword useless against Spaniards with rifles. As the Spanish fled, the backward-looking and history-struck Wheeler, leading the First and Tenth regiments of regulars, is reported to have shouted to his men, "The damn Yankees are on the run!"

This sharp and bloody battle lasted about two hours; it was over at a little after nine in the morning. According to initial counts, the attacking Americans lost sixteen dead, and fifty-two were wounded. The defending Spanish lost ten dead and had twenty-five wounded. Roosevelt calculated that the Rough Riders lost seven dead and so many wounded that they suffered about a quarter of the overall American casualties. Along with the earliest deaths now lay an Indian, a cowboy, and an unknown soldier.

Journalists sent reports to their American newspapers that Colonel Roosevelt had been a magnificent soldier—calm, cool, and keen of judgment, brave and heroic. Roosevelt had proved that he was a leader of men in war, as he had been in civilian life. His leadership in this first skirmish is often called brilliant.

From all accounts at the time, Roosevelt's men followed him with awe and affection. In turn, he was caring about them at all times. His keen political instincts and gentlemanly manners—his noblesse oblige—carried over from peacetime activities to the bloody battlefront. His jingoist image was blurred by his courageous military feats.

The Rough Riders, along with the army, rested for six days while the plan for the final assault on Santiago—which was now only seven to eight miles away—was formulated. It would be a full-fledged assault against the Spanish army of thirteen thousand men, with eight thousand expected reinforcements. Food supplies finally arrived for the Americans, and Roosevelt intended to get some for his starved men. On June 30, he practically commandeered eleven hundred pounds of beans, claiming that they were for the officers (according to army rules, the only ones entitled to the delicacy), and his hungry men feasted. That same day, Roosevelt was made a full colonel and given command of his regiment, as Leonard Wood was made general.

On June 30 the Rough Riders were ordered to march three miles through dense jungle terrain to the town of El Pozo, a task that took eight exhausting hours. They bedded down in the mud—it was the rainy season—and waited. At dawn the next day, July 1, the final attack of twelve thousand Americans began as one column of soldiers was sent to the far right to take a village and the rest of the men, with the Rough Riders in their own column, pushed forward in parallel flanks. The well-trained and armed Spaniards awaited them. On Roosevelt's fateful day, shrapnel rained down on the men, but only nicked the colonel on the wrist. Several troopers were killed.

Roosevelt's men fought alongside the regular cavalry, which was on foot. The Spanish hurled furious fusillades of artillery and rifle fire at the Americans. The dead piled up. While all the men were exposed to the murderous Spanish fire, Roosevelt moved along the line on horseback to give courage to the Rough Riders as they took cover, unable to fire back because the enemy was too far away. The blues were to the left, the right, and in front of the Rough Riders. Roosevelt's men faced Kettle Hill. He dismounted and awaited orders.

It had become a confusing and frightening battle. Finally, at one o'clock, Roosevelt was directed by General Samuel S. Sumner to advance his men along with the regulars to get into position to fire at the enemy. Once again, on horseback and fully exposed, Roosevelt spurred his men on. Finding the officers of the black Ninth Cavalry unready or unwilling to advance, he shouted to let his men pass through their lines to fight. So challenged, the younger officers of the Ninth took over the leadership of their troop, and they all joined the Rough Riders' offensive, fighting fiercely all the way.

Roosevelt found himself in charge of fragments of six cavalry regiments and two brigades. He was the senior officer commanding the highest point, and his men were ahead of the regulars. He galloped out in front, waving his hat to direct the men, as all went up Kettle Hill, a flanking outpost to San Juan Hill. Both hills surrounded Santiago, and were fortified and entrenched with Spaniards. A thin line of blue- and brown-clad soldiers advanced under fire, many meeting death and injury. At one point, Roosevelt jumped from his horse and led the soldiers on foot. At another, he killed a Spaniard with his bare hands. The men took on Roosevelt's audacity, as they breathlessly climbed higher and higher, fighting all the way. Roosevelt stayed at the head of the men, wearing a distinctive blue polka-dot kerchief tucked under his sombrero to keep off the sun. For the rest of his life, the colorful picture he made on this day would be the indelible symbol of his courageous leadership.

The soldiers broke through three successive Spanish defenses to get to the top of Kettle Hill. Near the pinnacle, they ran forward cheering. The Rough Riders and the black army soldiers of the Ninth took the hill, each claiming they were first. The Spanish continued a fierce resistance. Spanish trenches were filled with dead soldiers, but the colonial troops continued their desperate fight.

Despite the barrage of screaming bullets from the enemy, Roosevelt decided to rush the next redoubt, San Juan Hill, the last great obstacle before Santiago. His men, now intermingled with the black soldiers, surged forward. Roosevelt raced a hundred yards ahead, looked back and saw no one behind him because they had not heard his call. He returned, the men followed him, and they all advanced. In the melee, the colonel killed one Spaniard with his revolver, just as the ridge was taken. The battle of the hills was virtually over by four thirty.

The assault on San Juan Hill by army blues and brown-clad Rough Riders, the latter invisible in the high grass, is captured by Richard Harding Davis:

They had no glittering bayonets, they were not massed in regular array. They were a few men in advance, bunched together, and creeping up a steep, sunny hill, the tops of which roared and flashed with flame. The men held their guns pressed across their breasts and stepped heavily as they climbed. Behind these first few, spreading out like a fan, were single lines of men, slipping and scrambling in the smooth grass moving forward with difficulty, as though they were wading waist high through water, moving slowly, carefully, with strenuous effort. It was much more wonderful than any swinging charge could have been. They walked to greet death at every step, many of them, as they advanced, sinking suddenly or pitching forward and disappearing in the high grass, but the others waded on, stubbornly forming a thin blue line that kept creeping higher and higher up the hill. It was the rising tide. It was a miracle of self-sacrifice, a triumph of bull-dog courage, which one watched breathless with wonder. The fire of the Spanish riflemen, who still stuck bravely to their posts, doubled and trebled in fierceness, the crests of the hills crackled and burst in amazed roars, and rippled with waves of tiny flame. But the blue line crept steadily up and on. And then near the top, the broken fragments gathered together with a sudden burst of speed, the Spaniards appeared for a moment outlined against the sky and poised for instant flight, fired a last volley and fled before the swift-moving wave that leaped and sprang up after them.

Roosevelt was ordered to hold the line. He was now the highest-ranking officer still alive and in command of army men and his Rough Riders. He valiantly hung on, even while they were all desperate for blankets, shelter tents, and food. They dug entrenchments with Spanish tools and eagerly ate the cooked Spanish food they found. But all was still uncertain as the Americans sustained heavy casualties. Officers as well as ordinary soldiers had been killed.

Ten percent (205) of the American forces were killed; eleven were wounded. Roosevelt made a quick count of the Rough Riders: eighty-six were wounded or killed, and six were missing, with forty down with illness.

On the day of this fierce fighting, Roosevelt was recommended for the Medal of Honor. Meanwhile, Spanish troops were reinforcing Santiago before the coming battle for the last seven hundred yards.

The Spanish navy was destroyed by the Americans on July 4, effectively ending the war, although no peace treaty had been signed. The siege of Santiago dragged on for two weeks. Roosevelt fumed at American incompetence in the high command. He could do nothing but try to protect his men from disease and to feed and find medicine for them despite stiff army rules and regulations that made no sense to him. He wrote to Cabot about all this on July 19:

> Our condition is horrible in every respect. I have over one hundred men down with fever in my own camp out of my regiment of four hundred, 200 having previously died or having been sent to the rear hospitals. The mismanagement of the hospital service in the rear has been such that my men will not leave the regiment . . . yet we have nothing for them but hardtack, bacon, and generally coffee without sugar. I cannot get even oatmeal and rice except occasionally by paying for it by myself . . . I have to buy the men canned tomatoes and tobacco. . . . I feel terribly to see them suffering for lack of plain food, to see my men in high fever lying in the mud on their soggy blankets. . . . My men's shoes are worn through; two of them went into battle barefooted. Their clothes are in tatters. They have not changed their underclothes since they landed a month ago.

On July 17 the Stars and Stripes finally flew over Santiago. Roosevelt was now an acting brigade commander. Long and tedious negotiations with the Spanish had begun on July 3. The army had dug entrenchments around Santiago, and the navy had sunk most of the Spanish warships. The Americans did not want to level Santiago because of all the suffering the civilians would endure, so they issued an ultimatum, as truces came and went. The war had receded after July 10, but negotiations stalled once more. Then the Americans threatened to pour troops into Cuba—up to 50,000—and the Spanish capitulated on the condition that all their troops—23,500—could return to Spain.

At the end, Roosevelt counted 200 of his men lost and 123 of the survivors ravaged by fever. His command had taken the heaviest casualties of any in the expedition. He grieved over his huge losses. But to some antiwar critics he seemed callous about his men's lives. All told, 1,600 Americans had been killed or wounded in what John Hay, the secretary of state, called "a splendid little war."

In December 1898, Major General Leonard Wood wrote to the adjutant-general of the army in support of the initiative to grant Roosevelt the Medal of Honor. Wood's letter is, even today, the best nonpartisan account of the colonel's bravery ever written:

> Colonel Roosevelt, accompanied only by four or five men, led a very desperate and extremely gallant charge on San Juan Hill, thereby setting a splendid example to the troops and encouraging them to pass over the open country intervening between their position and the trenches of the enemy. . . . He gathered

up a few men and led them to the charge. . . . The charge in itself was an extremely gallant one, and the example set a most
inspiring one to the troops in that part of the line. . . . There
was no doubt that the magnificent example set by Colonel
Roosevelt had a very encouraging effect and had great weight
in bringing up the troops behind him. During the assault,
Colonel Roosevelt was the first to reach the trenches in his part
of the line and killed one of the enemy with his own hand. . . .
His services on the day in question were of great value and of a
most distinguished character.

Roosevelt did not get his medal, however, because he
was charged with interfering with the army's conduct of
the war. Because he was a volunteer soldier, and not subject
to army rules, some officers in the regular army had asked
Roosevelt to write to the president and to the secretary of
war, urging that the forces in Cuba be sent home after the
victory before disease decimated them. Russel A. Alger,
the secretary of war, seethed over this "insubordination."
Roosevelt had attacked him in his letters to Cabot, which
the Massachusetts senator used in his Senate speeches. Alger did not forget that affront. He had been pilloried about
the "mismanagement" of the war and he blocked the attempt to give Roosevelt a Medal of Honor. In fact, Roosevelt did not receive one until 2001, posthumously.

By mid-August the Rough Riders were home, and Roosevelt was buoyant about his "crowded hour," as he called it.
The war soon brought him even larger rewards than did his
mastery of men. He was now even more famous than the
president. Powerful men in New York were maneuvering to
restart his political career. And the wartime experience had

matured Roosevelt. He thought better of the average American man, and he gained experience in managing yet another organization.

In September, Roosevelt's First Volunteer Cavalry presented their commander with a Frederic Remington sculpture called the Bronco Buster. He responded to the honor by saying that he was proud of his regiment because it was an American troop composed of men of all the different races who had, either by inheritance or adoption, made America their country. He closed with a tribute to the brave black soldiers who fought with the Rough Riders.

CHAPTER 5

Man of the Hour

While on the whole I should like the office of Governor ... the position will be one of such extreme difficulty, and I shall have to offend so many good friends of mine. . . . I should have to treat with and work with the organization, and I should see and consult with the leaders. . . . I do not believe anybody would so much as propose to mention conditions to me. . . . In the last resort I should have to be my own master.

———

I do not believe that it is wise or safe for us as a party to take refuge in mere negation and to say there are no evils to be corrected. It seems to me that our attitude should be one of correcting the evils and, thereby showing that, whereas the populists, socialists and others really do not correct the evils at all, or else only do so at the expense of producing others in aggravated form, on the contrary Republicans hold the just balance and set our faces as resolutely against improper corporate influence on the one hand as against demagoguery and mob rule on the other.

———

I should be inclined to accept any honorable position; that the Vice-Presidency is . . . if I were a serious possibility for 1904. . . . What I should really most like would be to be re-elected governor with a first-class lieutenant governor, and then be offered the secretaryship of war for four years. Of course it would be even better if I could become United States Senator. . . . Secretary of War appeals to me most.

E VEN BEFORE ROOSEVELT RETURNED FROM Cuba, his friends began writing to him about running for governor of New York. He was the man of the hour, not only in the nation but also in his home state. In writing to Cabot in early September 1898, while he was still with his troops, he feigned indifference to getting back into politics:

> If I am nominated, well and good; I shall try to be elected, and if elected, I shall try to rise to the extremely difficult position in which I shall find myself. If I am not nominated, I shall take the result with extreme philosophy and with a certain sense of relief, and shall turn my attention to the literary work awaiting me.

Roosevelt knew that it would not be easy to get the nomination because Thomas C. Platt, the most significant power broker and the Republican machine boss, opposed him. Platt thought Roosevelt would not take orders; he knew in his bones that Roosevelt would want to lead. Again coining the metaphor that Roosevelt himself might have enjoyed, if it were not at his own expense, Platt told his followers that Roosevelt was the perfect bull in a china shop.

Besides the trial with Platt as an obstacle to his progress, there was Edith's reluctance to reenter public life. She soon became enthusiastic and even went to the state convention, held in Saratoga, New York, on September 27. A not inconsiderable factor in Roosevelt's calculation to bend toward politics was the governor's salary—ten thousand dollars, along with a free house in Albany. (Roosevelt later called it a gloomy mansion filled with cheap, hotel furniture.) And he mused again, in a letter, that he wanted to leave a legacy to his large brood of children. (Earlier, he had made his military service his legacy.)

Although Roosevelt flirted with the Independents—anti-Platt men and a mélange of reformers—he would run only as a Republican. He believed there was "a lunatic fringe to every reform movement" and that "ultra-pacifists" opposed him, but he had the support of "at least nine-tenths of all the sincere reformers." Roosevelt let it be known, in a private letter, that he would respect Platt's views on New York state affairs—he would consult him—and Platt did not try to block what became an inevitable Republican event.

Roosevelt was in the race. He took the nomination at the state convention by a margin of almost four to one. He then met with the president and Platt in early October, reporting to Cabot that "on the surface things seem to be going my way. Whether this is all mere froth I can't tell. Of course it is too early for a forecast that amounts to anything."

The campaign Roosevelt waged for governor was a phenomenon for a Republican, as it took the form of a populist crusade that only Democrats like William Jennings Bryan were known for. He ran a personal, emotional, press-the-flesh campaign throughout the state for over a month while wearing an extravagant hat reminiscent of his Rough Rider sombrero, which he waved wildly around. He had recently learned how to be a military fighter, and he brought that martial spirit into the political arena as he attacked the Democratic Party's candidate, Augustus Van Wyck. He stormed the political barricades as though he were still in Cuba fighting dangerous and wily adversaries. Like a good commander, he introduced the tactics of quick blitzkriegs of immense energy and colorful speeches in towns and cities. He gave more than one hundred speeches, sometimes nearly a score a day, as he rode the many well-placed railroads around the state. He was the most charismatic leader for public office the state had ever witnessed.

Here is one newspaper account of Roosevelt's political magic on the hustings:

> Wednesday, it rained all day and in spite of it there were immense gatherings of enthusiastic people at every stopping place. At Carthage, in Jeff. County, there were three thousand people, standing in the mud and rain. He spoke about ten minutes—the speech was nothing, but the man's presence was everything. It was electrical, magnetic. . . . When the train moved away, scores of men and women ran after the train, waving hats and handkerchiefs and cheering, trying to keep him in sight as long as possible.

Roosevelt's charisma went beyond the notice of New York even this early. A newspaper publisher in the West watched the new phenomenon and wrote of Roosevelt:

He is a rare combination of originality, unconventionality, candor, self-confidence, alertness, fearlessness, aggressiveness, positiveness, and nervous energy, and it is no doubt this combination which has made him the popular hero he is today.

There was also substance to Roosevelt's show. He cobbled together several general themes that resonated with the voters, as over and again, he bellowed that he trusted them. He called for honest government and an upright judiciary. He recognized the needs of laboring men—they would be a part of a philosophy of opening up opportunity for all. And he called for executive leadership. Roosevelt had had just enough experience in how legislatures worked in the dark and often under malign influences to know that they needed a strong governor to lead them.

In 1898, at the age of forty, Roosevelt was elected governor of New York by a slim margin. He summed up his life at that moment in uncharacteristically upbeat terms to a friend in a letter:

I have played it in bull luck this summer. First to get into this war; then to get out of it; then to get elected. I have worked hard all my life, and have never been particularly lucky, this summer I *was* lucky, and I am enjoying it to the full.

Roosevelt's admirer, John Hay, captured the mood of the victory when he wrote:

While you are Governor, I believe the party can be made solid as never before. You have already shown that a man may be absolutely honest and yet practical; a reformer by instinct and a

wise politician; brave, bold, and uncompromising, and yet not a
wild ass of the desert [i.e., a Democrat].

Roosevelt did not expect his luck to continue, but he
was content to be elected to his first statewide office. Becoming governor was his largest challenge so far in managing men, although it was not as daring as the military.
Certainly, Roosevelt meant to bring to bear all the various
lessons of his life and experience. He seized the mantle,
not caring if he ever held another office. His friends saw
his elevation as the salvation of the Republican Party in the
state because, as they told him, in private and in public, he
would be honest, practical, reformist, brave, bold, and uncompromising. The tributes were over the top. Now deeds
would count.

While waiting for his inauguration on January 2 of the
new year, Roosevelt wrote *The Rough Riders,* which was
published in 1899, although it was serialized first in *Scribner's Magazine.* The book was a huge success, although it is
a surprisingly modest account of his adventures in Cuba.
The journalists whom he had invited to cover the Rough
Riders' war had already made him heroic. Of course, some
differed with the mythmakers, among them Finley Peter
Dunne. Writing as Mr. Dooley, an Irish wit, he suggested
that the title of Roosevelt's book should have been "Alone
in Cubia."

Roosevelt was surprised when the Red Cross reim-
bursed him seven hundred dollars for the supplies and
food that he had paid for out of pocket for his men. The
colonel's family was now in its best financial shape ever.
Undoubtedly, this came as an immense relief to Edith,
who had worried constantly about money. She was the

family's accountant and also oversaw Sagamore's little farm at the Roosevelt homestead, which produced some income. Much later, Roosevelt's brother-in-law looked after the family's finances, but it is seldom clear from Roosevelt's own bookkeeping statements whether he truly knew about his income and expenses.

When Roosevelt became governor, New York was the most populous state, prosperous and industrial, with a big farming population. It led the nation in manufacturing and was a dominant player in the garment and dairy industries. And New York City, of course, was the financial capital of the country as well as home to a large and diverse immigrant community. Other large cities like Buffalo, Rochester, and Albany mimicked New York. More than half of the state's population lived in the largest cities, and one-quarter was foreign born. In western New York, prosperity depended in large measure on the Erie Canal, through which were shipped golden crops of grain from the nation's western states to the Atlantic Ocean. The state's railroads were also engines of wealth as shipping agents and modes of transportation for New Yorkers. With a population of more than seven million, New York was ever growing and making itself the workshop of the nation.

New York outstripped the capacity of its primitive governing institutions to manage the present, let alone the future. Mostly, political leadership had been left to second-rate governors such as the Republican John A. Dix and Democrats Samuel J. Tilden and David B. Hill. There was, perhaps, a single exception during this period, the Democrat from Buffalo, Grover Cleveland, who was governor from 1883 to 1885. Apart from Cleveland's tenure, it was the political parties that governed the state, in the absence of a permanent bureaucracy or of agencies or commissions. Parties used the immense patronage at their disposal to appoint their own men to run state affairs. The busy Erie Canal and the port of New York employed party men, for example. Because political parties were almost evenly matched in voting strength in the late nineteenth century, each election cycle led to intense political struggles for spoils and power.

Roosevelt's challenge was to get around the 1894 Constitution, which made the legislature—thoroughly dominated by the majority political party—all powerful and the governor little more than a figurehead. Those constitutional fathers, however, never dreamed of the whirlwind coming on that would mightily shake the structure. Roosevelt understood the status quo. As governor, he intended to burst the seams of the Constitution's garment. He meant to be a strong executive who would make policy and manage the government, who would tackle the new industrial order. He knew that he had to create a new kind of politics to succeed. In his words, he would strive for efficiency, honesty, morality, principle, duty, courage, character above all, and common sense. He planned to bring to his tasks, additionally, persuasion and publicity. A foreign observer saw Roosevelt at the time as "reason made hot by passion."

Jacob Riis, the preeminent reform journalist in New York and a great admirer of Roosevelt, was ecstatic upon the new governor's arrival in Albany. "The whole big state shouted with us," he wrote. "Theodore Roosevelt was Governor, elected upon the pledge that he would rule by the Ten Commandments. . . ." The new chief executive did not disappoint his admirers, as he delivered a short and memorable inaugural address to the legislature on January 2, 1899. Roosevelt intended to get done all the things that were left undone by a recalcitrant legislature when he was a three-term assemblyman.

Roosevelt's annual message, delivered on the heels of his inaugural, was more specific and expansive. He touched on the excesses of the new capitalism of large corporations and their financial benefactors, whose synergy amassed immense wealth, some of which bought political favors. He wanted to assist the laboring man caught up in what seemed a social Darwinism, a survival of the fittest. He intended to protect watersheds and the environment from pollution and keep lands pristine for wildlife. Roosevelt wanted to make taxation more equitable, clean up politics by uncoupling party machinery from business tribute, and replace an incompetent judiciary. A uniform civil service was also a goal.

Roosevelt's language in this first message revealed the man thinking out loud on governing:

> There is much less need of genius or of any special brilliancy in the administration of our government than there is such homely virtues and qualities as common sense, honesty, and courage.
>
> All that can be done is to face the facts as we find them, to meet each difficulty in practical fashion, and to strive steadily for the betterment both of our civic and our social conditions.
>
> In the long run, he serves his party best who most helps to make it instantly responsive to every need of the people, and to the highest demands of that spirit which tends to drive us onward and upward.

Roosevelt got along well with Boss Platt, who often met him in New York City to hash out goals and procedures. Platt liked to think of himself as a schoolmaster to politicians. If Henry Adams, distant heir to two presidents, thought Platt would "cut Roosevelt's throat," the lamb was not brought to slaughter. Roosevelt reveled in being in Albany, which he saw as a "little English cathedral town." "It is rather good to be here," he wrote. He viewed himself as a regular "republican." He worked with his party when he could, or slid out from under it when necessary. He attracted new followers with his inspired publicity. He used his popularity as a force within and outside his party and always spoke plainly.

He began coining memorable phrases as spurs to ambition: "Let us live in the harness. Let us rather run the risk of wearing out than rusting out. The virtue worth having is the virtue that can sustain the rough shock of actual living." All his life, words would be weapons for a people yearning for the great romances of their history, which, after the Civil War, were fading.

How did the young governor think of his progress? He wrote to a follower:

So far things have gone along very smoothly. . . . Senator Platt [who had made himself U.S. senator] and I have had to step on several matters in which he, on behalf of the organization, was greatly interested; but he has been most kind and most considerate. In return I have been scrupulously careful to tell him exactly what I intend to do and not to go back one hair's breadth on my word in any case. For the first five weeks, therefore, we have gotten along very well. Of course I shall have difficulties

ahead of me with the machine on one side and the idiot independents on the other, but I am fortunate in the fact that I am
not trying to build up a machine for myself and that I am letting the question of a re-nomination take care of itself.

Roosevelt's two-year term was for him a period of ex-
hortation and continual thinking about the proper content
of politics. One thousand bills were passed by the legislature and signed by the governor, and five hundred languished or were rejected. He said he was often exhausted
by the work because nothing escaped his attention. He was
tireless in talking to legislators, leaders, and prominent
personages. He brokered arrangements, traveled the state,
held press conferences twice a day of fifteen minutes each,
and sought advice from stellar academic experts. He wrote
hundreds of letters, many even on international affairs,
which he never slighted.

Roosevelt's signature battle was for a bill that would, for
the first time, tax franchises that had received grants from
the state, at no cost to them, to provide public utilities—
gas, electric, water, and transportation. These lucrative
grants soon became immense engines of personal fortunes—as well as of political bribes. After a titanic fight using shrewd politics, Roosevelt was successful, much to the
infinite dismay of financiers like J. P. Morgan and machine
politicians. The franchises were now taxed as real estate by
the state, the taxes on them yielding $11.5 million that could
be spent on state needs. Roosevelt knew a great triumph
when he won it. "We have on the statute books the most
important law passed in recent times by any American
State legislature," he recorded.

Boss Platt charged that the franchise tax issue would deliver New York City to the Democrats, who opposed it. (And he was proved right.) During the struggle, Roosevelt tried to calm Platt down by explaining that he sought "moderation," or a kind of golden mean, on tax issues. Platt would have none of it. He fought Roosevelt "bitterly and frantically," in the governor's words. When he lost, Platt began scheming for revenge against Roosevelt, who was smashing his china shop of cozy arrangements between legislators and corporations.

Governor Roosevelt took on large corporations and trusts by seeking to make them report their profits. He sought laws to break monopolies and to oversee accounting reviews to get corporations to pay their taxes. Not incidentally, he thought he made corporations more moral by making them pay their fair share. Roosevelt also knew corporations would now have less money with which to corrupt politics. Legislators were still being bought, either to favor laws to assist corporations or to desist from introducing laws to injure them, the latter a kind of blackmail.

Within the broad sphere of society and social relations, Roosevelt preferred order, regularity, and balance. This meant curbing the meretricious, laissez-faire tendencies by business that had injured the laboring population. The way to help labor was to empower it to organize and even strike, although Roosevelt would never condone mob violence either by labor or capital. Labor was expected to negotiate wages and conditions.

Boss Platt was not a convert to Roosevelt's ideas on political economy. Before Roosevelt became governor, Platt let it be known that he was "too altruistic" on economic matters. Platt called the colonel "impulsive" and "a little loose on the relations of capital and labor, on trusts and combinations." A standpat conservative Republican, Platt did not want his party to become populist, in the mold of William Jennings Bryan, that is, to embrace the movement that had emerged from the Kansas-Nebraska bill in 1854. (That law had to do with slavery extension. It established the principle that the people, and not a legislature, would decide a political issue. It led to conflict and mayhem.) The Democrats expanded this concept of popular sovereignty to economic matters in the late nineteenth century, and a Populist Party had emerged in 1892 that favored letting the people, instead of elected officials, decide issues. It was a direct threat to Republicanism and their tight control over political agendas.

On labor questions, Roosevelt got not only an eight-hour day for state workers but also an increase in factory inspectors to enforce laws already on the books against tenement sweatshops. He happily signed a bill to require licenses for the repair or manufacture of goods in any basement or tenement. Thereafter, licenses were to be granted after inspections showed that space and light were adequate. He did not get increased liability for workers injured in industrial accidents, which were becoming alarmingly too frequent.

Roosevelt favored better labor conditions because he believed the interests of the workingman were those of all citizens. Labor issues provided a great challenge to Roosevelt as governor, as they would when he became president. When labor called strikes, Roosevelt acted when there was a possibility of violence. He readied the militia three times but never used it. These conflicts concerned hours of work and pay. In one case, Roosevelt himself thought wages were too low. Conflict broke out on the Buffalo docks, among street railway employees in New York City, and among workers at the Croton reservoir outside New York City. Mediators from Roosevelt's department of labor were usually called in to look at such situations, and they normally settled the disputes skillfully. Records show that of the 547 strikes or lockouts in 1900, for example, 225 were mediated and 46 were settled with state help. There are no records of the outcomes of strikes in which the state was not involved. Roosevelt's position in all this was as much to help labor assert its legitimate needs as to better the administration of state government. Government was an active force. This primer on labor was carried into Roosevelt's presidency.

It was not extravagant for Roosevelt to characterize the reconciling of the divisions between capital and labor as the great domestic challenge of the day. He did not want working men to be socialists or to favor the Democratic radicalism of the populist William Jennings Bryan. Republicans ought to recognize the wrongs in the capitalist system and bring a balance to a classical economic regime. In his words, "There is a great growth of economic unrest among the laboring classes in the east, who show a strong tendency to turn to Bryan, simply because they are against the established order and feel bitterly because of wrongs which are really inherent in the nature of things, and not in the least due to any party policy."

The governor's labor policies ran parallel to his concerns about political jobs. When his reformed civil service—a second triumph as governor—received a large percentage of state jobs, perhaps 20 percent were given out on the basis of written tests, not politics or race. And when enforcing legislation dealing with jobs, he was not swayed by a person's creed, color, or nationality. Just as he had done when he was civil service commissioner, Roosevelt acted on the belief that every man should be treated according to his merits.

When Roosevelt got his civil service bill, he was opposed by his friends, and he felt bitter about it. And he was "saddened . . . that the great bulk of the people continue so utterly indifferent or even in a lukewarm way hostile to the civil service law." He wrote that he had never in his life "had to work for anything quite as hard . . . to get . . . the civil service law passed." That it was the politicians and not the reformers who stood by him to pass such a controversial bill was a revelation. Reformers wanted perfect bills; Roosevelt crafted bills that could pass, even if not in "exactly the shape" he wished, as he put it. He was fast becoming a practical politician and slipping away from the high idealism of reformers. His hard political life seemed to mimic, more and more, the strenuous life he knew in the saddle, and his resilience owed much to his experience with the ebb and flow of the natural world in the West. If Roosevelt rose like a rocket, he governed like he was shot from a gun.

Roosevelt's civil service reforms remained largely unappreciated not only by party bosses but also by blacks. He was particularly baffled by the lack of enthusiasm among blacks for him as governor because he thought he had done more for them than any other officeholder. Black opposition started when, in considerable numbers, they opposed him for office, the first Republican gubernatorial candidate to be so spurned. What was going on? It is clear that Roosevelt did not recognize that the tie forged between blacks and the

Republican Party during the bloody Civil War was beginning to fray. Jobs, not nostalgia, motivated blacks. The Democratic Party doled out jobs for votes, and this trumped the Republicans' waving of the bloody shirt, which was supposed to remind blacks that Republicans had fought a desperate Civil War to free black slaves.

Roosevelt's broad attention to social concerns included education. The governor wanted to improve education, and he signed legislation to give higher salaries to New York City teachers. He believed that schools at all levels needed improvements, and he included the state university. Significantly, he also opposed a local option that could segregate schools—his own children, he declared, attended racially mixed schools in Albany. The new-century politician, so well educated himself, understood how important education was in the evolving society.

Just as Governor Roosevelt wanted to help blacks, he also sought to protect women. He eased prison conditions for them because the system was built more for men. But he refused to stay the execution of a woman for murder, believing, once more, in equal treatment for the sexes. He did seek a better method of hanging, however, as he did not want another woman, or anyone, suspended by a rope around the neck for fifteen minutes before expiring. A broken neck, and not strangulation, was more humane, he thought.

Roosevelt was ahead of most of the country on women's rights. He had always favored suffrage for women. In college he wrote a paper that a feminist might have penned. He believed that women and men were equal, especially in marriage. (He hedged a bit on that conviction, however, after he married and had children, preferring that women claim domestic duties as their equal role to a man's providing for his family.) He was generally welcoming to the rising woman's movement for broader rights and consulted with women leaders in the new social movements.

With measured success, Governor Roosevelt fought two battles aimed at getting a better-administered state government. He negotiated with Platt to improve appointments to boards and state offices. Political machine candidates were rejected before they could be ostracized. (One predecessor, the Democrat Grover Cleveland, also had a good record on appointments.) More important, Roosevelt worked to clean up the immense corruption connected with Erie Canal repairs. Nine million dollars had been allotted to canal expenditures, and the immense sum of $1 million was lost in overcharges or skimmed by corruption. Roosevelt resolved the canal issue by bringing in a "body of experts," who were engineers, men of business, and especially transportation experts of all kinds. Roosevelt saw to it that more honest men were put in charge of the canal work and that public work was run along better business lines, with less involvement of the political machine in drawing up contracts. He also got a handle on the general administration of the canals for the whole state. Once more, the scientific and data-driven politician cut the pattern for strong leadership.

Conservation was another Roosevelt triumph during his time as governor. The early naturalist and lover of the outdoors, the romantic writer about the West and all nature managed to create a huge preserve in the Catskill Mountains. Never bashful, he told the legislature that "the Forest Preserve will be a monument to the wisdom of the founders." He also tightened laws to prevent loggers from devastating sylvan areas, and he stopped pollution in the Saratoga area by fiat. The keen administrator also replaced the political deadheads on the state's fisheries, game, and forest commission. In his autobiography, he recollected that "all that later I strove for in the Nation in connection with Conservation was foreshadowed by what I strove to obtain for New York State when I was Governor."

What is striking about Roosevelt as governor was his intention to educate eastern Republicans to the needs of the new world around them, with its high industrialism, spread of urbanism, globalization, and dominant laissez-faire doctrines. He was in the vanguard of forward-looking, progressive politicians. A patrician who inherited his father's philanthropic sensibility toward the impover-ished, the governor sensed that more was needed beyond the philanthropy of previous generations. The problems were so vast that only the government could resolve them with positive action. Always, Roosevelt kept an open mind about how to meet them. He consulted with reformers who had studied conditions in the state and had offered solutions in articles and books. He even read the works of the most impassioned reformers, whom he called muck-rakers, because of their attack mode of writing. But they brought his and the nation's attention to issues needing immediate reform, such as purer food and drugs.

The reformers' crusades would bring action when Roo-sevelt was president, since Boss Platt's Republicans as well as the Democrats were not receptive to much progressive legislation. Then, too, the rigidities and peculiarities of politics in New York prevented too much gubernatorial in-novation. Roosevelt's work on the frontiers of modernity was isolating him, as the Republican Party remained pliant to Platt. As 1900 dawned, Boss Platt put into motion his secret plan to get back his state from the Albany dynamo. He would make Roosevelt vice president and express him to Washington.

Roosevelt was riding so high as governor and was so sanguine about the future that he challenged Americans publicly to follow the philosophy he called "the strenuous life." He coined the phrase in one of his most memorable speeches on April 10, 1899, in Chicago, before the Hamilton Club. It helped make him the exhorter-in-chief and the owner of a bully pulpit. With a few words, he burnished his already iconic image as a man of high morals and strong character:

> In speaking to you, men of the greatest city of the West, men of the state which gave to the country Lincoln and Grant, men who preeminently and distinctly embody all that is most American in the American character, I wish to preach, not the doctrine of ignoble ease, but the doctrine of the strenuous life; the life of toil and effort; of labor and strife; to preach that highest form of success which comes, not to the man who desires more easy peace, but to the man who does not shrink from danger, from hardship or from bitter toil, and who out of these wins the splendid ultimate triumph.

What is important about Roosevelt's governorship is his continuing attention to the progressive ideas that emerged during his earliest office holding. His thinking was on the glide path of progressivism that was smoothed by pragmatic action. Roosevelt was no bomb thrower.

When he acted, it was in a moderate way on behalf of a reformist agenda. A historian at heart who revered the early fathers of the republic—and wrote books and numerous essays about many of them—he wanted to scrape off the evil excrescences of the times and reaffirm old values while offering necessary new ones. The new century demanded higher standards for all.

Roosevelt's short tenure as governor was an apprenticeship for his later career, although at the time he hardly thought he had a future in politics. In 1900 he was measured not in grand accomplishments but by some reforms, along with vision, ideas, hopes, driving energy, and a genius for publicity. He said at the time that one must dare to be great, and no one could accuse Roosevelt of not being bold.

As governor, he made the state regulate capital and labor. Individual needs were made less free, as a result, before the community's needs. Roosevelt's worldview began to emphasize the community over the individual. His later programs while president, which took the names Big Stick, Square Deal, and New Nationalism, were grand extensions and applications of Roosevelt's years as governor.

At the turn of the century, Roosevelt was happy to be governor. He wished to run again and finish his work—two years were hardly enough to accomplish much. He believed there was no way to even try to be president before at least 1904, so he idled his political motor. What to do? Roosevelt decided he could be content as a family man until the political clouds lifted. He was certainly blissfully happy and just as much enraptured with his wife as he ever was. He never thought his second marriage was anything but a "love match." He wrote in a letter at the time:

There is nothing in the world—no possible success, military or political which is worth weighing in the balance for one moment against the happiness that comes to those fortunate enough to make a real love match—a match in which lover and sweetheart will never be lost in husband and wife. . . . I am just as much devoted to Mrs. Roosevelt now as ever I was.

Then the hand of fate, not his own exertions, pushed Roosevelt onward. The New York Republican machine had had enough of Roosevelt's independence and progressivism. And so Platt executed his secret plan in Washington in late 1899. He concluded a bargain with the Republican power brokers in the Senate to make Roosevelt vice president. The die was cast. He told politicians that "Roosevelt might as well stand under Niagara Falls and try to spit the water back" as to stop his nomination. In a more profane moment, Platt admitted that he wanted "to get rid of the bastard." Senator Mark Hanna, an ultimate power broker, screamed out, "Don't any of you realize that there is only one life between this madman and the White House?" His complaint fell on deaf ears. When he warned, "We are not going through this campaign with a high colored vest as the tail of the ticket," he was ignored. Another politico lamented that Roosevelt was a "cowboy" and "undignified." It all went unheeded. Roosevelt would be kicked upstairs.

Roosevelt was himself opposed to his elevation, when the rumor mill began to whirl in December 1899 and into the new year, because he thought the vice presidency a useless office. He said so to Cabot and Platt. In letters to friends and family he said that he preferred other kinds of offices, if he could not run again as governor, ranging from secretary of war, to governor of the Philippines, to U.S. senator. Platt at first denied he had a secret plan, but he was furious when Roosevelt caught him lying. Cabot wanted Roosevelt to be vice president, but he was not part of any cabal. When Roosevelt learned of the power behind the push to get him out of New York, he knew he could not stop the momentum. The plutocrats, the machine, and the independents were too strong to fight. So he let it happen.

This did not mean that Roosevelt welcomed his coming elevation. He worried, once more, about his finances. In 1899 and 1900 he was well off, thanks to his governor's salary and writings. However, he thought that the vice presidency would be a "serious" drain and would cause "Edith continued anxiety about money." Vice presidents of late entertained lavishly, something he could not afford to do. How would it look?

Roosevelt was ambiguous about the vice presidency, even as the national convention got under way in late June 1900. He entered the auditorium late, after proceedings had begun, but then he gave up the ghost when he wore a large black, broad-brimmed hat, reminiscent of the sombrero he wore during his Cuban exploits. One wit intoned, "Gentlemen, that's an Acceptance Hat."

How did Roosevelt feel about his elevation? He told Cabot, "Instead of having to fight single-handed against trusts and corporations, I now must take pot luck with the whole ticket, and my anxieties on behalf of the nation are so great that I can say with all honesty there . . . [are] none left." He added that "Edith is becoming somewhat reconciled."

Roosevelt rose to the occasion and carried the fight to the public. He ferociously took on the Democratic candidate, William Jennings Bryan, who stood for all that Roosevelt and President McKinley did not. While McKinley did not campaign, as was the custom, but stayed on his back porch in Canton, Ohio, Roosevelt traveled over twenty-one thousand miles and visited twenty-four states and nearly six hundred towns and cities. He made almost seven hundred speeches. Three million people greeted him.

Roosevelt's main message to the people on his whirl-wind tour was to stay the course. What McKinley stood for in 1896 was still right for 1900. It was said of the president that he had grasshoppers in his ear, so close did he hold it to the ground. The chief executive knew the American people. And he was popular and steady. On the hustings, Roosevelt expanded on the words he spoke at the national convention on June 21. Republicans gave men the opportunity to prosper. "American energy, opportunity, and thrift" made the nation the most prosperous ever. In foreign policy the nation had overthrown a "medieval despotism" at its door in a brilliant war, in a "struggle for righteousness." The Republicans had passed wise laws and thwarted a "Populist Democracy" of "shame, disgrace, and business chaos."

Several of Roosevelt's campaign speeches were more specific on the issues of the day that separated the parties, and his language was livelier. He took on the call Bryan made once more in a presidential campaign (he had also run in 1896) for an end to the gold standard, the Republicans' cornerstone of prosperity. On September 7, 1900, in Michigan, Roosevelt said that "Mr. Bryan's financial policy . . . [was] utterly ruinous." Bryan's views were "figments of disordered brains." The Democrat, it was said, "coos as mildly as a sucking dove when he whispers his unchanged devotion to free silver" and was criticized for being also in favor of "fiat [paper] money." A "sound and stable" currency was needed for prosperity, Roosevelt argued. Only "demagogues" argue differently.

Roosevelt charged that Bryan stood for "the doctrine of some men down, and our doctrine is all men up." He decried "class hatreds" being stirred up and called for a return to Washington's and Lincoln's doctrines of "orderly liberty under law."

Roosevelt defended the Cuban war. It was central to the honor of the United States, as the Civil War was in 1864 when Lincoln, seeking a second term, fought for "the honor and interest of our common country."

The United States was also in a guerrilla war against the Philippine insurgent, Emilio Aguinaldo. Roosevelt asserted that neither in 1864 nor in 1900 was the war about imperialism.

The prospective vice-presidential candidate attacked Bryan for "the most shadowy ghost that ever was raised to frighten people—the ghost of militarism." Roosevelt retorted that the army was too small to be a threat. In a speech on October 12, 1900, in Evansville, Indiana, Roosevelt took on the Democratic Party's challenge to a larger standing army. Lincoln had asked for, and received, a large army. Then, as now, the people would decide the question, Roosevelt said. At Madison Square Garden on October 26, 1900, Roosevelt accused Bryan of "the disbursement of the army, the dishonor of the flag, and the contraction of natural limits."

In his speeches, Roosevelt exhorted "each generation to do its allotted task," as the fathers of the Civil War had done. He wrapped the Republican platform in past and heroic deeds, while defending present-day programs. Over and over, he exhorted his listeners to attend to the bright future on the horizon of a new century and not to look back to Democratic darkness and regression. Roosevelt, the great phrasemaker and forecaster, would elevate the turn-of-the-century political battle to one between Bryan's longing for the past and Roosevelt's challenge to the future. It was a choice between the nineteenth and the twentieth centuries, a small-farmer republic or a clanging industrial order.

Roosevelt became vice president in March 1901, at a salary of eight thousand dollars, but without a free house. On November 6, 1900, he and McKinley had won a smashing political victory, the greatest since 1872, when General Grant had swamped his adversary. The Electoral College tabulated 292 votes for the Republican to 155 for the Democrat. The popular vote for McKinley-Roosevelt showed the margin of victory to be three-quarters of a million.

Roosevelt, the once-reluctant candidate, was initially right about the office of the vice president being one of near stagnation, a place with little to do. He presided over the Senate for a few days in March 1901 to approve appointments. Then the Senate adjourned until December, when the newly elected Congress would open for business.

On September 6, 1901, Roosevelt was hiking in the mountains when McKinley was shot by an anarchist in Buffalo, where he was attending the Pan-American Exposition. Roosevelt was called to the president's bedside, and at first there were hopeful signs that he would recover. By September 10, the vice president had returned to his retreat. But McKinley took a bad turn and died on Friday, September 13. Called back to Buffalo for a second time and under grievous strain, Roosevelt was sworn in as president of the United States the next day. At age forty-two, he was the youngest man ever to hold the office.

"Now that damned cowboy is in the White House!" bellowed an anti-Roosevelt Republican. But Roosevelt would soon demonstrate that his several and varied careers had been a preparation, an education, for a larger and more significant political role. The aspects of his experience—of family, class, eastern and western exposure, wartime service, a set of principles, tested policies—would join in a heady concoction that became Republican progressivism. In nothing less than a revolution, Roosevelt would make reform and character, which had been the polestars of his hero, Abraham Lincoln, acceptable once more to the Republican Party. The new president never doubted that progressive Republicans were Lincoln's heirs, and he would use the martyr's heritage to exhort, challenge, and change the nation. He would be midwife to a new birth of Republicanism.

CHAPTER 6

The Accidental President

The two great fundamental internal problems with which we have to deal (aside from the problem of mere honesty, social and governmental . . .) are the negro problem in the South, and the relations of capital and labor . . . to one another and to the community at large.

All thoughtful men must feel the gravest alarm over the growth of lynching in this country, and especially over the peculiarly hideous forms so often taken by mob violence when colored men are the victims—on which occasions the mob seems to lay most weight, not on the crime but on the color of the criminal. . . . It is of course inevitable that where vengeance is taken by the mob it should frequently light on innocent people. But even when the real criminal is reached, the wrong done by the mob to the community itself is well-nigh as great. Especially is this true where the lynching is accompanied with torture. . . . Whoever in any part of the country has ever taken part in lawlessly putting to death a criminal by the dreadful torture of fire must forever have the awful spectacle of his own handiwork seared into his brain and soul. He can never be the same man.

I have won my leadership purely by an appeal to what I think I may, without priggishness, call the conscience and the imagination of the people. I depend for my nomination and election upon there being a general sentiment that the character I have shown in handling the Panama business, the post-office scandals, Cuban reciprocity, the Philippines, the anthracite coal strike . . . the Northern Securities case, the Alaska boundary case . . . the upbuilding of the navy, etc., etc., entitles me to leadership and to popular confidence and support.

"IT IS A DREADFUL THING TO COME INTO THE Presidency this way," Roosevelt wrote to his friend Henry Cabot Lodge, the Boston Brahmin senator. "Here is the task, and I have got to do it to the best of my ability." Roosevelt had become president after McKinley was assassinated on September 14, 1901. This was the third presidential assassination in less than fifty years. The murderer was an anarchist called Leon Czolgosz.

Roosevelt took the oath of office in borrowed clothes, looking sartorially splendid nevertheless, having traveled by carriage and special train through rain and mud from his mountain retreat to Buffalo. He was sober-looking and dignified but nervous and tense, as he stepped up to the presidency. After taking some food, visiting, then consulting with cabinet members and others, he fell into bed, exhausted. When he revived he announced, "I feel bully."

The colonel was probably the best-known politician in the country, having been a military hero and in public life since the age of twenty-three. His ebullient personality, varied talents, war record, and reputation as a reformer—although a not wholly successful one—in an age of acute conservatism made him a popular figure.

Roosevelt publicly and properly mourned McKinley's demise, and he pledged to Republican leaders that fateful day in Buffalo that he would follow in the martyr's footsteps. In his private letters he referred to himself as an accidental president, and he knew he had no mandate of his own. Roosevelt calibrated his initial decisions so that the great and powerful Republicans, who ran the country, would give him a chance. When Senator Mark Hanna of Ohio reached out to him on October 12, for example, Roosevelt responded, "It would not be possible to get wiser advice than that contained in your letter of the 12th and I shall act exactly upon it. I shall go slow, and do nothing until I have had a chance to consult you."

Everyone knew Roosevelt was a man of action, however, and the new president, although trotting in McKinley's path, had polestars of his own to guide him in national politics and in world affairs. In his private letters, public writings, and actions, Roosevelt began setting out a clear vision of how he intended to be president. He meant to govern. He would establish the presidency as a vital force and make it the equal of the then all-dominating Congress. And he wished to update the Supreme Court to make it more responsive to people and less attentive to property rights. His presidential model was Lincoln:

> I must not only be as resolute as Abraham Lincoln in seeking to achieve decent ends, but as patient, as uncomplaining and as even-tempered in dealing, not only with knaves, but with the well-meaning foolish people, educated and uneducated. . . .

And I must show the same spirit in painfully groping to find out the "right" course.

At first, Roosevelt decided to behave and act cautiously. He knew many viewed him as a tempestuous person because of his war exploits and fiery words as a reformer and governor. He kept on McKinley's cabinet. They included Secretary of War Elihu Root, Attorney General Philander C. Knox, and his friend, Secretary of State John Hay. Roosevelt wrote of his early months, "In the little work, the easy work, of these days of peace and prosperity, I see on a small scale much what Lincoln saw in the supreme years of the nation's struggle."

Above all, however, he relied on his earliest political ally, the astute senator he called Cabot, as a sounding board. Their letters are a treasure trove for understanding Roosevelt's presidency. For seven years, and until their principled break in 1908, Lodge's affection and admiration for Roosevelt were legendary. Before anyone else, he had seen greatness in him, and he now rejoiced in his friend's rise to eminence. Lodge had become a personal as well as a political intimate, the kind of ally all presidents need and few ever have. Those who did not have them, history has shown, have fared badly.

The new president did not throw caution to the winds, but boldly tacked in domestic and foreign affairs. He saw his office as a powerful and almost unrestrained vehicle for positive government on behalf of the people. In his autobiography he recaptured these moments:

The most important factor in getting the right spirit in my Administration, next to the insistence upon courage, honesty, and a genuine democracy of desire to serve the plain people, was my insistence upon the theory that the executive power was limited only by specific restrictions and prohibitions appearing in the Constitution or imposed by the Congress under its Constitutional powers.

Roosevelt would "speak softly and carry a big stick." But to get anything done well, he intuitively knew that he would have to make himself the head of the Republican Party, for it ruled in Congress and, prior to his presidency, the nation. The Senate was the key, and it was tightly controlled by Senator Hanna and his followers within the states. Since state legislatures, not voters as yet, chose senators, there was an unbroken and unchallenged line of power in the party. Hanna and Republican barons used the vast federal patronage to raise money and get out the Republican votes. Spoilsmen were taxed and were the foot soldiers at election time. In order to be the powerful president he aimed to be, Roosevelt had to challenge the Republican leadership on the distribution of the immense federal patronage, estimated at tens of thousands of jobs, mostly in the post offices and the ports. He would have to be the only dispenser of the loaves and fishes. His plan would not countenance timeservers, who were political hacks. In order to lead and administer the government, Roosevelt would need his own chosen men. He planned to keep on honest persons and to appoint the best new men and women, regardless of party or color or ethnic origin.

Roosevelt explained his hiring standards in a letter to Clark Howell, the editor-in-chief of the *Atlanta Constitution*, a Democrat who was recommending Republicans for office, saying that "the prime tests . . . applied have been those of character, fitness and ability." He further stated that when he could not find a suitable Republican office-holder, he chose a Democrat. As he explained, "I cannot treat mere color as a permanent bar to holding office, any more than I could so treat creed or birthplace."

Roosevelt concentrated on the South in reforming the Republican Party because he viewed it as the most corrupt and racist section in the country. During McKinley's first term, Boss Mark Hanna "secured the appointments of very bad negroes in office to keep the black delegates [to Republican national conventions] solid," the president observed. Hanna then kept "the white men in line by refraining from touching in any way upon the fundamental ethical elements of the situation." Roosevelt would have none of this kind of governance, if he could help it.

Roosevelt took pains to explain his policy in personal letters to Southerners, seething at the change. He chose a "fit . . . colored man," as he put it, for the important post of collector for the port of Charleston and another for collector for the port of Savannah. At the same time, he removed a black postmaster in favor of a white appointee in South Carolina. "Why the appointment of one should cause any more excitement than the appointment of the other I am wholly at a loss to imagine," he wrote to a complainer. He also expressed surprise when questions about "social equality" and "negro domination" were raised. "To connect either of these appointments [in Charleston and Savannah] . . . with such questions as 'social equality' and 'negro domination' is as absurd as to connect them with the nebular hypothesis or the theory of atoms," he retorted. For Roosevelt, political equality was not an open door to social equality, which he regarded as a private matter and a choice.

*President Roosevelt in 1903, addressing
African-Americans in Summerville, South Carolina*

Southern Republicans went from a slow simmer to a
full boil on the patronage distribution. Roosevelt hoped
he could turn down the fire. He consulted state and local
party leaders, House and Senate magnates, and those he
deemed "gold," or "sound," Democrats on patronage matters. (The acceptable Democrats were President Cleveland
types and not Bryan followers, who wanted paper money
not backed by gold. The gold standard limited the supply

of money and made it expensive at a time of economic expansion, and it kept prices high.) He also called on the most famous and admired black educator, Booker T. Washington, to help him scout honest black and white appointments, Republicans and sound Democrats. In a letter, Roosevelt reported that he and Washington "agreed that in the Gulf and South Atlantic States, where unlike what is the case in Tennessee and North Carolina, there is no real Republican organization which has any particular effect at the polls, the thing to do would be freely to recognize Democrats and try to appoint men of the highest character—Republicans where they were available, Democrats where they were not; and to appoint a very few colored men of high character—just enough to make it evident that they were not entirely proscribed." Roosevelt put good administration of the government above the Republican ascendancy in the South. It was a brave decision that would haunt and injure him in 1912, when he battled his party for nomination for a "third" term.

The patronage brouhaha reached a crescendo when Roosevelt invited Washington to dinner at the White House. Southerners lost all restraint in attacking him. On October 16, 1901, the *Memphis Scimitar* screamed, "The most damnable outrage which has ever been perpetrated by any citizen of the United States was committed yesterday by the President when he invited a nigger to dine with him at the White House."

Headlines in southern newspapers included racial slurs like "Our Coon-Flavored President." The unexcelled racist, Senator Benjamin R. Tillman of South Carolina, threatened in a speech that "a thousand niggers in the

South would have to be killed to teach them 'their place again.'"

Roosevelt was more than nonplussed by the reaction. He explained his motives to an admirer on October 24 in a personal letter:

> As to the Booker T. Washington incident, I had no thought whatever of anything save of having a chance of showing some little respect to a man whom I cordially esteem as a good citizen and good American. The outburst of feeling in the South about it is to me literally inexplicable. It does not anger me. As far as I am personally concerned I regard their attacks with the most contemptuous indifference, but I am very melancholy that such feeling should exist in such bitterly aggravated form in any part of our country.

To Cabot a few days later, he lamented:

> I regard its sole importance as consisting in the view it gave one of the continued existence of that combination of Bourbon intellect and intolerant truculence of spirit, through much of the South, which brought on the Civil War. If these creatures had any sense they would understand that they can't bluff me. They can't even make me abandon my policy appointing decent men to office in their own localities.

Roosevelt scribbled to another follower within the week, "That idiot or vicious Bourbon element in the South is crazy because I have had Booker T. Washington to dine. I shall have him to dine as often as I please." But, of course, he did not. The race issue had become so explosive that southern Republicans were allying themselves with Democrats on the wedge social issue of protecting racist policies and practices. Roosevelt always maintained that he did nothing wrong, in any sense, as indeed he had not, but he bowed to the racists. Henceforth, he would be advised by Washington without having him to dine. At the same time, Roosevelt had blacks to dinner, and stay over, at his Oyster Bay house without notice or a furor. In the White House he did not give up on showing openness to the races, as when in 1903 the Roosevelts entertained Episcopal bishops, clergymen, doctors of divinity, and deacons, with their wives and daughters. Among them were two "negroes," and "nobody shrank from them," Roosevelt reported.

Roosevelt did not neglect how patronage was distributed outside the South. He paid attention to the activity throughout the country and "established a rule of conduct" that became "universal." From his autobiography we know that he tackled the issue of reform in this prime party function. His inquiry found that "the offenders were confident and defiant because of their great political and business backing." He appointed an investigator to seek out the "unscrupulous" who were shielding offenders and gave him "support" and a pledge of no "interference."

"An appalling amount of corruption" was "unearthed," Roosevelt recorded. He withstood "the yells of anger from all directions" at him and persevered. "Several convictions, including convictions of the most notable offenders," took place. He was satisfied that "the worst offenders were sent to prison, and the remainder dismissed from the Government service. . . . The corruption was completely eradicated." When some politicos complained that the scandal would hurt Republicans, the resolute president replied in a letter: "I did not believe it would hurt the party. It did not hurt the party. It helped the party."

ALMOST FROM THE TIME of his ascendancy as an accidental president, Roosevelt was concerned about the 1904 presidential election. A satisfactory patronage distribution was a part of any winning strategy, of course, along with the passage of reform laws. Of all the states needed for a successful coalition, his home state was most important. "It was very nearly out of the question that a man can be nominated with his home state against him, and it is practically certain that my State will be against me," Roosevelt wrote Cabot in late 1901. He also watched as two rival Republicans, Boss Platt and Benjamin Barker Odell, a rising politician, fought for control of the Republican Party. Odell found that Platt had lied to him and would not be his ally.

During the struggle, Platt told Roosevelt that he would favor him continuing on as president, but Roosevelt did not put much stock in this because he thought Platt, who was not well, would be ousted by 1904. Still, Platt stuck to his plan, and he believed Odell would be more likely to follow him than would Roosevelt. The president calculated that the West and New England appeared ready to back him for the nomination, but "when he [Platt] acts in cold blood he would probably oppose him."

Odell was put up for the governorship of New York, which he won, so Roosevelt succeeded in knocking together the competing heads of the state Republican Party. Now the two giants would have to work together. At the time of the rapprochement, a ditty published in a newspaper summed up the triumph:

He (Roosevelt) had taken each of them under an arm,
They could neither budge nor shout an alarm—
"I want you, peace being dear to me
To be the staunchest of friends," said he,
"In foul as well as in pleasant weather—"
Their heads as it happened were bumped together—
"In peace, dear friends, let us ever dwell,"
He gently advised them as they fell
And when they recovered, all was well.

Roosevelt declared Odell a good governor, as he did not undo his reforms and even followed in his steps. Still, he was less successful than Roosevelt in getting along with Boss Platt, probably because he did not give as much deference to Platt's dignity as he required. Furthermore, Odell was not as open to the Boss about his plans as was Roosevelt, who used to meet Platt in New York City most Sundays to attend his political school. Hidden tension continued.

Almost immediately on Roosevelt's becoming president, men of finance like George W. Perkins, a Morgan partner, visited Roosevelt to ask him "to do nothing at all, and say nothing except platitudes" about trusts, and not demand information from corporations as a "right." In a letter the president asked his brother-in-law, the businessman Douglas Robinson, to look over a draft of the trust part of his forthcoming annual message for December 1901, and possibly let Perkins know about it. A few days later, Roosevelt wrote again to Robinson, "Perkins might just as well make up his mind that I will not make my message one hair's breadth milder. . . . Perkins simply represented the effort to sit back in the harness. . . . Such effort was worse than useless."

Clearly, and from the beginning of his presidency, Roosevelt was going to be challenged by the greatest economic powers in the country, who had had their own way in driving the economy for years and who viewed him as a threat to their ownership of the nation. Republicans had allowed their party to run roughshod over the government and labor on behalf of corporations, but Roosevelt, who considered himself "conservative" generally, was not going to be quiet about illegal monopoly power. In 1890, monopolies had been outlawed by the Sherman Antitrust Act, which was often forgotten in practice. Roosevelt intended to scrutinize trusts and make them follow the law. He had demanded accountability from corporations when he was governor of New York, when they overvalued stock, watered stock, and fooled investors with corrupt practices, and he would take his battle against what he called "bad" trusts to the larger playing field.

The great trust issue also had a political dimension. Roosevelt was not going to let economic barons run the country. He believed in the supremacy of federal power over both the economic system and the states, some of which had antitrust laws. And the president intended to be the arbiter among contending economic powers and the supreme political leader in the country. In his first annual message to Congress on December 3, 1901, he pointedly asked for laws for compulsory publicity and increased supervision by the national government over corporations in interstate commerce. "Great corporations," he said, "exist only because they are created and safeguarded by our institutions; it is therefore our right and our duty to see that they work in harmony with them as institutions." His words were mild and measured, but to all who knew his record of curbing trusts in New York when he was governor, they were warning enough to the new moguls of the new century.

The first test of Roosevelt's policy on trusts came in 1902, when he challenged the Northern Securities Company, a large combination of businesses that formed a trust. It was in "restraint of trade" and illegal. (A trust was defined at the time as a vertically integrated set of businesses that controlled all aspects of production and distribution.) The Northern had combined a number of railroads in the West to dominate and to control all traffic. Roosevelt estimated that Northern stock was watered down by one-third in the merger. It was engaging in bad conduct.

The Northern Securities case stunned big business and financiers—even though straws had been in the wind—because the president did not alert business interests beforehand. J. P. Morgan, the greatest financier of the age, let it be known—in a soon-to-be-famous statement of business-as-usual arrogance—that if anything wrong had been done, his man and Roosevelt's ought to meet and fix it. Morgan added that, if he had been warned of Roosevelt's proclivities, he would have dissolved the combination rather than contravene the Sherman Antitrust Act. Roosevelt was incensed by Morgan's suggesting a man-to-man, behind-the-scenes negotiation when the public's good was at stake. Business could not stand on equal footing with the federal government in settling disputes. Roosevelt spurned Morgan's cozy suggestion. A New York journalist, picking up on the new political climate, dismissed Morgan's offer as ludicrous and maliciously lashed out with the

*President Theodore Roosevelt using
the Bully Pulpit in New England, 1902*

comment, "Wall Street is paralyzed at the thought that a President of the United States would sink so low as to try to enforce the law."

It took two years, until 1904, for the Northern case to wend its way toward a Roosevelt victory. The trust had broken the law, and the Supreme Court agreed with Roosevelt when he acted to dissolve the world's second largest trust. The president, on behalf of the nation, not the industrialists and financiers of Wall Street, was going to police the most powerful economic engines in the country.

Roosevelt also aimed at the business practices of railroad corporations behaving badly. These iron horses, which distributed tons of farm products and goods, were owned and run by industrialists and financiers who favored insiders in setting rates and gave secret rebates to friends. In 1904, Roosevelt asked for a reform of rate setting, and he repeated his call the next year. He had his attorney general take action against railroads giving rebates, and the government won several suits. He then introduced a bill in the House that embraced his reform. After a fierce battle in the spring of 1905, with Roosevelt leading a coalition of Republicans and Democrats in the Congress (a coalition of both parties was unheard of in past years), and with threats to call for high inheritance taxes to tame the new industrial buccaneers if the railroad reform was rejected, progress was made.

By May 1906 the Hepburn Act, which advanced railroad regulation, passed. Roosevelt got what he sought, though less than what more radical reformers demanded. It was to him "a fine piece of . . . legislation, and all that has been done tends toward carrying out the principles I have been preaching," he pronounced in a letter. He would later ask for an improvement in the act to plug a vital loophole. He wanted the Interstate Commerce Commission to evaluate railroad property in order to determine proper rates. Along the way, the Congress passed the Elkins Act, which prohibited rebates to favorite clients. (Railroaders had already reached a point at which they did not want to give these anymore!)

Roosevelt instituted a broad program to regulate all large companies operating across states. His Department of Justice went after other firms restraining trade, including the American Tobacco Company, the Union Pacific Railroad, the beef trust of Swift and Company, and Standard Oil, among others. Before rebates were outlawed, Standard Oil had been fined severely for giving rebates, although a judicial decision reversed this the next year. Within a year, and then continuing into his presidency, Roosevelt, and not big industrialists and financiers, was dictating the terms of the workings of many of the essential elements of the nation's political economy. Not incidentally, and at about the same time, he attended to labor's place in the new strategy. It was put at the same level as business and under federal supervision.

The first big test of the federal government's role as arbiter in clashes between capital and labor came in May 1902, when an anthracite coal strike broke out after problems had been simmering for some time. About one hundred forty thousand miners, mostly immigrants, demanded recognition of their union, a pay raise of 10 percent, a shorter workweek—the miners worked twelve-hour days, six days a week—and a more honest weighing of the coal they dug, which was the basis for their earnings. They had secured a 10 percent pay hike two years before, but that had already been eaten up by the rising cost of living. The miners were also angry that they had to buy their food and rent their miserable shacks from the companies. They even had their pay docked for medical expenses. A miner earned $560 a year, which would translate into about $7,800 in today's money.

Even though powerful men like Morgan, Elihu Root, Cabot Lodge, and Mark Hanna sought to broker a settlement, the six coal-carrying railroad companies dominating the negotiations refused to budge on any issue. The chief spokesman for the owners, the troglodyte George F. Baer, said the workers were not suffering. "Why, they can't even speak English!" he declared. Baer also uttered the instantly infamous words: "The rights and all interests of the laboring man will be protected and cared for—not by the labor agitators—but by the Christian men to whom God in His infinite wisdom has given the control of property interests of the country." The public sided with the workers and, even after 100 years, their cause seems just.

Roosevelt monitored the situation, which grew even graver, when calls went out from businessmen to cite the union for restraint of trade. Then the weather became a factor. The northern parts of the country would soon be out of coal, as the winter loomed. He needed to reach out to all parties, but under what rubric? He wrote to Hanna in September, "I don't see what I can do, and I know the coal operators are especially distrustful of anything which they regard as in the nature of political interference. But I do most earnestly feel that for every consideration of public policy and of good morals they should make some slight concession." To Cabot he wrote that he could not find any legal way to intervene:

> Unfortunately, the strength of my public position before the country is also its weakness. I am genuinely independent of

the big monied men in all matters where I think the interests of the public are concerned, and probably am the first President of recent times of whom this could be truthfully said.

He would not do favors for the big moneymen and so he could not expect anything in return. "I can make no private or special appeal to them," he opined. Roosevelt thought the owners thick-skulled, and, surprisingly, Morgan thought them foolish.

The coal operators began to discern that even if they did not accept Roosevelt's view that they had a duty to aid the public, and not just to line their pockets; at least the federal government, personified by the president, was an active player in the political economy. By early October, Roosevelt wrote in a personal letter that the operators of the coal mines "cannot assume that theirs is a private business, on the contrary by their action they are jeopardizing the whole system of private management of the coal fields and are rendering it likely that drastic action will be taken in the way of authorizing governmental regulation of their work." The president was being radicalized toward the notion that some essential businesses were as much public as private in their services. Horrifically, by this point, $46 million of coal receipts had been lost; $28 million of transportation income was gone; and workers had lost $25 million in wages.

Roosevelt foresaw a dangerous coal famine in the winter. It would be "ugly" with "terrible suffering and a grave disaster." At one point, he even thought he might have the army seize the mines in order to have coal dug. "I am up to my ears in the coal strike business," he wrote to a western newspaper owner, William Allen White. "I get a good idea of Lincoln's worry at the time when bodies representing on the whole a majority of the people were about evenly divided in denouncing him because he did not go far enough, and because he went too far." To another correspondent, Roosevelt wrote, "In this present crisis it is curious to see exactly the same tendencies of the human heart coming to the front. Just as Lincoln got contradictory advice from the extremists of both sides at every phase of the struggle for unity and freedom, so I now have carefully to guard myself against the extremists of both sides."

After much strenuous effort from many quarters, with Roosevelt in the lead, a commission finally settled things, with miners getting their raise of 10 percent and a nine-hour day but no union recognition or better coal weighing. (Not surprisingly, the price of coal went up 10 percent.) Roosevelt won a victory for the power of government, if not fully for the miners or consumers. He kept the union from being destroyed. But, just as important, he put government above capital and labor as an honest broker. In this test of his presidency, Roosevelt declared that he acted "for the public welfare. . . . The needs of the Nation demanded" action, and he provided it in a new way. Hitherto, presidents broke strikes with soldiers. Now, a president stood above the actors and guided change with intense negotiation between parties. During this contentious period in the history of the rising industrial economy, Roosevelt did, and did not, intervene in industrial strikes. The triggering factor for intervention was the possibility of violence. In the next year, 1903, he sent troops to Arizona mines, although he did not use them, and he did not order military action in a Colorado mine dispute (the state had stepped in.) Roosevelt readied troops during a strike on Chicago's rails, but they were not deployed.

Union unrest and managerial hardness led to Roosevelt's refining his labor position at about this time. He let it be known that, while he favored unions, he preferred the open shop, where all persons could work in a union setting, over the more prevalent closed-shop model. Significantly, he added that not color, ethnicity, or creed should interfere with the chance of getting a job in a unionized company. The labor wars showed Roosevelt that it would be the duty of the president to be the "steward of the people," to do whatever is constitutionally acceptable to respond to their needs.

PRESIDENT McKINLEY plunged the country into world affairs with the Spanish-American War and into the clutches of imperialism, as Spain, the defeated and once-grand power, ceded lands to the American victor and suffered Cuba's independence. It was Roosevelt, however, who fashioned a policy that extended and amplified what was a limited McKinley program. The new president was a well-read and strategic thinker ready to practice the art of diplomacy, and the situation in 1901 in the Caribbean and Pacific provided an almost perfect stage for him to enter as the leading man with a large role. He told the Congress in his first annual message in December 1901 that the nation had "rights" in the world and "duties" to perform. Cuba was free but would be protected by the United States from foreign interference. In effect, he was signaling that the large island would be under America's defensive shield. Latin America was screened off from European interference by the 1823 Monroe Doctrine, which stated that European countries

would not be allowed to interfere in the affairs of these republics, and the nation's new empire in the Pacific, especially
the Philippines, would be a territory under U.S. suzerainty. It
had been liberated from Spain but would not be allowed to
be independent because it was not ready. Roosevelt wanted
to avoid anarchy and bloody conflicts if the army was with-
drawn. The civil government and religious and educational
institutions would suffer. He rejected what he called a "policy
of scuttle." It would be "morally indefensible."

But the denial of self-government had touched off a
bloody insurrection in the Philippine Islands under
McKinley, and the revolution also gave new life to the
anti-imperialist movement of Republicans, Democrats,
and reformers, who had opposed the war and now rejected
the elements of the peace.

Roosevelt inherited the bloody Filipino war. The
American army was winning the battle against the guerrilla forces of Emilio Aguinaldo, the revolutionary leader,
but stories of brutality by the army stunned the nation.
The army already knew some cruel ways from the Indian
wars, but new kinds of torture horrified Americans. One
particularly vicious tactic was the "water cure." A gallon of
water was forced down a prisoner's throat and then his ab-
domen was beaten until his belly burst or he died. Then,
too, General Jacob H. Smith ordered his men to take no
prisoners of Filipinos over ten years old, and he intended
to make one large province a "howling wilderness."

In letters to complaining correspondents, the new
president wrote that he did not "like torture or needless
brutality of any kind," and, at a Memorial Day speech in
1902, he promised to find the torturers and punish them.
That same month, an outraged Roosevelt had contacted

Taft, the governor of the Philippines until 1904, to appoint a commission to look into the conduct of the army toward Filipinos. Secretary of War Root was also tracking events.

In his mind, Roosevelt once more looked back on Lincoln's presidency for justification of his actions on the Filipino question. In 1904, he shared what had been his thinking on the issue with the Congress. He declared that forty-four years ago the "Republican party was dedicated to freedom. . . . It has been the party of liberation and emancipation from that hour. . . . It broke the shackles of four million slaves, and made them free, and to the party of Lincoln has come another supreme opportunity which it has bravely met in the liberation of ten millions of the human family from the yoke of imperialism." So, in the young days of his presidency, and to rally his party, Roosevelt had substituted the image of the bloody shirt for the spread eagle. The martyred President Lincoln was made a man for all reasons.

Roosevelt used Taft's and Root's reports on the conduct of the army in the Philippines in his annual message to the Congress on December 2, 1902. He declared that there were "individual instances of wrong-doing," and that "the culprits were found and punished." He had discharged offenders and had installed new military leadership. The former brave soldier would not allow the army to disgrace itself and behave in un-American and unmanly ways.

Roosevelt did not, in any way, defend the cruel behavior of American troops. Good historian that he was, however, he noted that Americans had done worse in the past in Indian wars in the West. All of this Roosevelt put on record in a letter to Elihu Root, the secretary of war:

The accusation that there had been anything resembling systematic or widespread cruelty by our troops was false. . . . In the Philippine Islands the task had been a thousand times more difficult and the provocation to our soldiers a hundred times greater, and yet nothing had occurred as bad as . . . [the] massacre . . . at Wounded Knee.

At that massacre twelve years before, Roosevelt recalled, "squaws, children, unarmed Indians, and armed Indians who had surrendered were killed, sometimes cold-bloodedly, and with circumstances of marked brutality." It was no consolation, of course, that the army was behaving a notch above its worst recorded behavior in warfare. Roosevelt, however, thought it important to mention its slightly more civilized way of war.

On becoming president, Roosevelt ordered that all civilian appointments to the Philippines were to be made without any political consideration of any kind. The islands were to be made ready for self-government, with sanitation improved, railroads and roads built, and a public school system put into place. His greatest problem, however, and a great cause for the Filipino war, was land ownership. Roosevelt tackled the tricky issue with ingenuity, while holding back complaining American Catholics with patience. The Spanish Catholic Church controlled immense amounts of land, about four hundred thousand acres, on which sixty thousand peasants toiled. The workers claimed their rents were too high. The Catholic priests, or friars, had also taken it upon themselves to establish local governments, and reputedly they were notoriously corrupt and frequently immoral. Aguinaldo warred against the church, the friars, the landholders, the miserable local government, and the immorality of the padrones.

Roosevelt charged Taft to broker a deal with the pope, who, as head of the Roman Catholic Church, owned all the friars' lands in the Philippines. It was not until 1903 that the difficult problem of landholding was settled. The pope sold the church land held by the friars to the United States for fewer dollars than the president originally offered the stubborn Vatican. The Spanish friars were allowed to stay in the Philippines, although most left. Roosevelt saw that the land was then distributed to Filipinos, beginning the creation of a small-farmer nation. By 1908, Roosevelt turned over to Taft, his successor, the most progressively governed colonial territory in the world. He never got much credit for his Philippine victory, however, because it was overshadowed by the atrocities committed by the American army.

During 1902, Roosevelt was under intense fire by political opponents of all kinds, but especially from Democrats on the Philippine question. He struck back by trying to change the subject. He made a deliberately inflammatory public statement about lynching by fire, which was more abhorrent than what the American army was accused by Democrats of doing in the Philippines. He bellowed, "Whoever in any part of the country has ever taken part in lawlessly putting to death a criminal by the dreadful torture of fire must forever have the awful spectacle of his own handiwork seared into his brain and soul. He can never be the same man again." The South was experiencing an orgy of lynching in recent years, and white southerners were furious with Roosevelt for calling attention to their horrific crimes.

Of course the South did not take this attack lying down. Southern editors and politicos responded. One journalist wrote:

> He . . . condemns lynching negroes who outrage our womanhood. . . . He is a narrow-minded bigot . . . [a] modern Judas . . . [a] prostitutor who smites the South. . . . Burning and hanging negro rapists is a terrible crime in the eyes of this would-be Caesar. . . . This is the low estimate President Roosevelt places on the virtue of our women.

During 1902, several more foreign policy questions received Roosevelt's attention. The Alaska boundary issue with Canada was settled within a year, as England nodded toward the American position. Then Roosevelt turned to the Monroe Doctrine when troubles brewed in Latin America. He wrote:

> I regard the Monroe Doctrine as being equivalent to the open door in South America. That is, I do not want the United States or any European power to get territorial possessions in South America but to let South America gradually develop on its own lines, with an open door to all outside nations, save as individual countries enter into individual treaties with one another.

Roosevelt could foresee "transitory intervention" on the part of any state outside of South America when there was a row. But he was wary of German intervention and kept an eye on England's powerful and roving naval fleet. Historically, England had been the covert enforcer of the

Monroe Doctrine because it also did not want Europeans playing in Latin America. But an instance arose in which England was involved in a Latin American crisis, arousing Roosevelt's interest. Venezuela could not pay its debts to foreign powers, mostly Germany and England.

Roosevelt rejected the notion, put forth by Germany, of a collaborative action in Latin American crises. Later, to John Hay, he recorded what he had concluded at that time:

> The American people will never consent to allowing the American Republics to come under the control of European powers by such subterfuges as exercising this [syndicate] control under color of a protection to the guaranteeing or collecting a debt.

Making things more difficult for Roosevelt to manage the trouble in the Caribbean in 1902 was the reality that the English were repositioning their navy around the world. In order to meet possible new threats from rising naval powers like Germany and Japan, they were gradually withdrawing their powerful fleet from the Caribbean for other stations. Realizing that England's new geopolitical strategy left the United States naked in its neighboring seas, Roosevelt decided on negotiation.

Roosevelt did not trust Germany's claim that it intended to bombard only Venezuelan ports and, with a few troops, seize custom houses to get the import duties it was owed. The president asked the German government to submit to arbitration or face an American battle fleet in Venezuelan waters. When nothing happened, he gave Germany twenty-four hours to accept arbitration, or he would send orders to Admiral Dewey to sail. At that point, England decided not to support Germany. An unspoken English-American entente seemed at work, isolating Germany. Ultimately, the international tribunal at The Hague settled matters.

Roosevelt exercised his "transitory intervention" in a more forceful way in 1902 when turmoil broke out in Santo Domingo, an island coveted over the years by Spain, France, and England. It had a history of revolution and of strong black leadership against imperial powers, with little stability or good government. The cause of the latest problem was its typically late debt repayment, in this case to Germany, Italy, Spain, and Belgium. Then, Dominican insurrectionists fired on an American cruiser. Not surprisingly, American property owners asked Roosevelt for protection, and the redoubtable Admiral George Dewey was sent by the president to scout the problem.

The trouble at Roosevelt's front door and the dangers posed by European imperialists led in May 1904 to a formal statement: the Roosevelt corollary to the Monroe Doctrine. It held that the United States would protect and would regulate the countries of Latin America and would not allow Europeans to interfere. While the corollary was forming in Roosevelt's mind, he took over customs duty payments to Santo Domingo; a part of the money was used to settle debts and build schools and roads. Even after these beneficial expenditures, the money returned to the government of Santo Domingo was the highest amount that benighted country ever had in its treasury. Once more, Roosevelt had forced good government on an underdeveloped nation. As was becoming customary, however, there was opposition to his interventionist doctrine.

To Elihu Root in June 1904, Roosevelt summed up his recent thoughts and actions on the expanded Monroe Doctrine and on its opponents:

> If we are willing to let Germany or England act as the police-man of the Caribbean, then we can afford not to interfere when gross wrongdoing occurs. But if we intend to say "Hands off" to the powers of Europe, then sooner or later we must keep order ourselves. What a queer set of (absent-) evil-minded creatures, mixed with honest people of preposterous shortness of vision, our opponents are.

Getting the Senate to agree to the corollary was not easy for Roosevelt. In his December 1904 annual message to Congress, the president took on all comers who were protesting his foreign policy. Once more, Roosevelt defended himself by going on the offensive against his adversaries, mostly Democrats in the South. He made his opponents look at their own "sins" before attacking him for his policies. He challenged them "to war against" the "sins of our own" before passing resolutions about wrongdoing elsewhere. "Civic corruption," "brutal lawlessness," and "violent race prejudice" needed to end in this country. The corollary did not gain approval until 1907.

The centerpiece of Roosevelt's strategic thinking in international affairs, a mindset that encompassed the protection of America's far-flung interests and a strong and modern navy, was put into place when he made possible the building of the Panama Canal. By any standard, it was an undertaking of immense historic, scientific, and engineering significance. It stands alone as a federal government development until the making of the atomic bomb in the 1940s and man's spacewalk on the moon in 1969. The canal would permit the navy to move from one ocean to another in three weeks instead of two or three months in order to respond to any threats to the mainland.

A French company had tried to build a canal through Panama in the late nineteenth century, but it met with defeat on the wings of the malarial mosquito, which felled most of the twenty-two thousand laborers and left the French with huge debts. Roosevelt had thought that a route through Nicaragua was better for a canal, but after a volcano eruption there, he backed away. When American engineers suggested that the Panama route was suited for transit, even though the French had met with stunning defeat there, Roosevelt, a man of science, backed them in 1903.

The process by which the Panama Canal was made possible is not entirely clear even after all these years. There were conspirators in Colombia working to get Panama to break away so that a route could be offered to the United States. They got just the chance they looked for when Philippe Bunau-Varilla, the super-energetic and fussy chief engineer of the defunct French company, and now a heavily invested spokesman for the New Panama Canal Company, joined with William Nelson Cromwell of the top international law firm of Sullivan & Cromwell on Wall Street. They furthered the "revolution" and shaped the financial outcome. They besieged Congress and even contacted men in the cabinet.

Publicly, Roosevelt acted as if he did not want to know the particulars of what was occurring at his doorstep. In his private view, Colombia was "a wildcat republic." He offered to buy Panama, but the corrupt and slippery Bogota government could not decide on what it wanted. To those who urged him to intervene, he "cast aside the proposition . . . to foment the secession of Panama." He preferred to wait for the time to negotiate a treaty rather than secure Panama by "underhanded means."

On September 15, 1903, an exasperated president wrote to his secretary of state, John Hay, to give his state of mind:

> In some shape or way, the United States would . . . interfere when it becomes necessary so as to secure the Panama route without further dealing with the foolish and homicidal corruptionists in Bogota. I am not inclined to have any further dealings whatever with those Bogota people.

Roosevelt would await the outcome of the revolution that would detach Panama from Colombia. In 1902, Congress had passed the Spooner Act, authorizing the president to acquire title of the New Panama Company "with its rights, privileges, franchises, and concessions in the Isthmus of Panama." For Roosevelt, the fruit had to fall from the tree first.

The conspirators declared Panama independent on November 3, 1903, and Roosevelt recognized the new nation with unseemly haste. The United States signed a treaty giving it a six-mile strip of land to build a canal. In exchange, it gave ten million dollars to Panama. An additional forty million dollars went to the new canal bondholders, Frenchmen, and others. Their names were never specified nor have they been discovered subsequently in any records.

The revolution in Panama was both a comedy and a dark drama of ineptitude that showed that there was neither a master plan nor a master at the helm. The revolt itself had cost one hundred thousand dollars paid from Bunau-Varilla's own pocket. Much of the money went to the Colombian army. The Colombian general was paid thirty thousand dollars in cash for sitting on his hands. His officers each received ten thousand dollars to stay in place. Soldiers, who did not exceed five hundred in number, were paid fifty dollars in gold for remaining idle.

The overt role of the United States consisted of the American navy lurking in the Panama area, ostensibly to protect America's interests. At one point, some Marines were landed on order of the on-site commander. At another point, in a quite unplanned act, an American railroad employee may also have played a key role. He kept a small contingent of Colombian soldiers, either honest or not yet bribed, from getting into Panama by denying them access to the American railroad that crossed the isthmus.

Roosevelt was only on the outermost edge of the crazy quilt of the revolution. He was neither the strategist nor the tactician of the Panama revolt. (It would have been a smoother operation, had he been actively involved.) Nor did the president instigate the revolution. In all that transpired, the badly organized revolution started and stopped at least twice and rambled along. The elements were not coordinated, and American military and consular officials were often inept, out of touch with each other and with events, and they acted in an ad hoc manner. At almost any point, the revolt could have failed. The Panama operation was basically a ragged coup assisted by the pluck of a few Americans on the scene, acting with no orders from Washington. Bunau-Varilla had a provisional government waiting in the wings and gripped a written constitution in his claw.

The anti-imperialists' opposition to Roosevelt's Panama interest reached a fevered pitch in the fall of 1903. Roosevelt responded, loftily, that he had acted in the national interest to recognize Panama and sign a treaty. His reasoning did not mollify critics, however. Because Roosevelt believed that he had acted legally and constitutionally in the Panama affair, he wanted his cabinet to support him, on behalf of his presidency and their party. But at a cabinet meeting in 1904, after the Panama treaty was signed, his advisers were jocular, when not hurtful. Attorney General Knox, tongue in cheek, advised, "If I were you I would not have any taint of legality about it." Secretary of War Root added mischievously, "You have shown that you were accused of seduction and you have conclusively proved that you were guilty of rape." In later years, Roosevelt, in one of his untethered fits of exuberance, declared, "I took Panama." But it was a misreading of events then, as it is now.

Roosevelt's geopolitical, military, and international policies, from the moment he became president through the several years until 1904, were the products of a coordinated strategy he had been constructing for years. "A party fit to govern must have convictions," he wrote to the elderly Speaker Joseph "Joe" Cannon on September 12, 1904. He had them in abundance, although he was decades younger. In his foreign policy initiatives he lived up to the Constitution in "letter and spirit," he asserted. "But the Constitution must be observed positively as well as negatively. The President's duty is to serve the country in accordance with the Constitution." Roosevelt believed in positive, active governance. It was a new day in the history of a still-new kind of nation. The voters would decide in November 1904.

EARLY IN HIS PRESIDENCY, Roosevelt made his mark in two areas of public life that would have more lasting consequences than, arguably, anything else he did. One was in the conservation of resources and the other in the molding of the Supreme Court. They were both vivid pieces of his progressive mosaic that was part natural and part human. Roosevelt was our earliest and most passionate environmentalist. He attended to nature's beauty and bounty, that is, to the country's natural resources and their protection and wise use. His scientific bent and western adventures— he thought of himself as much a westerner as an easterner—gave him a capacious and loving view of pristine forests. Those struggling to make a living on arid land, mostly west of the Mississippi, also caught his attention. Bringing water to the desert could advance intelligent development. Nature's gifts—its timber and underground minerals—could be harvested in ways that kept lands from depredation.

Congress had already preserved twenty-six million acres of land, but it allowed unabashed exploitation of them. President Cleveland had tried to halt the loose landleasing system that allowed people to use, but not own, federal land, but McKinley had reopened the federal lands for sale. In a matter of a few years, three million acres reverted to private hands.

At first, Roosevelt stopped selling off federal land to private developers. More important, he initiated significant changes in the many aspects of a conservation program. Select cutting of trees was mandated to stop the denuding of forests. New engineering works were begun to store water in dams in order to irrigate desert lands for farmers and ranchers. In 1901, Roosevelt thought "the Forest and water problems . . . [were] the most vital internal problems of the United States." In his first annual message to Congress on December 3, 1901, he laid the foundation for the development of irrigation and forestry, which he carried out for the rest of his presidency.

Roosevelt worked on a bill that became the Newlands Act in June 1902. A reclamation law, it set aside the monies from the sale of public lands for the purpose of reclaiming "waste areas of the arid West by irrigating land otherwise worthless, and thus creating new homes upon the land," in the president's words. Settlers repaid the monies to the government, and a revolving fund was set up. Roosevelt tried to get Speaker Cannon to go along with the measure, but, he quipped, "Not one cent for scenery." Probably in deference to Roosevelt though, Cannon allowed the bill to get to the floor. He led twenty-four Republicans against the measure, as it passed. Within a few years, twenty-eight projects were undertaken in fourteen states, and three million acres were irrigated to serve thirty thousand farms.

Roosevelt also pointed out in his first message that the Bureau of Forestry, under Gifford Pinchot, who was soon to become a legendary conservationist, needed reorganization, and all forests, west and east, needed study and a program. The resources of sixty million acres of national forest were opened for "regulated use" in a few years. At the same time, sixteen million acres of timberland were saved before "land grabbers" could get at them, the president recorded in his autobiography. When Roosevelt left office, nearly a half-million acres of agricultural land in the national forests had been opened to settlement. The ideal of the "Executive . . . [as] the steward of the public welfare," in Roosevelt's words, was stamped in history. The progressive Republican

President Roosevelt with John Muir at Yosemite, 1903

senator from Wisconsin, Robert La Follette, proclaimed at the time, "The Conservation of our Natural Resources . . . is probably the greatest thing Roosevelt did, undoubtedly."

The second Roosevelt action in 1902 that was highly personal and had large consequences beyond his presidency was the appointment of Oliver Wendell Holmes, Jr., to the Supreme Court. Holmes already had a brilliant career as chief judge of the Massachusetts Supreme Court. Roosevelt abhorred government by injunction, as he called it. The high court was antilabor, probusiness, laissez-faire to the extreme, and prohibited most union activity. In doing so, it put private property above individual or community rights, which Roosevelt thought was wrong. He wanted someone who was sympathetic to his views and had a progressive record on the great issue of capital versus labor. Holmes had shown himself no particular friend of big business and even displayed a tendency toward understanding labor. He had a progressive record and fell into Roosevelt's circle. Most important, Holmes did not view the law as remote, but as lived experience.

The president wanted an appointee of the stature of John Marshall, the nationalist Founding Father, whom he admired. He defended his choice in a letter this way:

> He has been a most gallant soldier, a most able and upright public servant, and . . . a citizen whom we like to think of as typical of the American character at its best. . . . [He] has been able to preserve his aloofness of mind so as to keep his broad humanity of feeling and his sympathy for the class from which he has not drawn his clients. . . . Holmes's whole mental attitude . . . is such that I should naturally expect him to be in favor of those principles in which I so earnestly believe. . . . He is not in my judgment fitted for the position unless he is a party man, a conservative statesman . . . and keep[s] in mind . . . his relations with his fellow statesmen who in other branches of the government are striving in cooperation with him to advance the ends of government. . . . [For example] the Supreme Court of the sixties was good exactly in so far as its members fitly represented the spirit of Lincoln.

Once on the court, however, in a minority opinion in 1904 on the major case that Roosevelt had used to practically launch his presidency in 1902, the Northern Securities Case, Holmes sided against Roosevelt. His objection to the majority opinion bitterly disappointed Roosevelt. It was one more instance in the history of the court of the unpredictability of appointments. Just as Marshall had stunned even the Federalists with his finding that judicial review resided in the Constitution, so Holmes refused to accept the common law as a set of fixed principles. He later dissented in key decisions, striking down a key labor law and a child labor law, protected First Amendment rights, and would not let the Fourteenth Amendment to the Constitution be used to prevent social experiments. For him, the Constitution was a living document, and not a finger on the dead hand of history. He was ultimately viewed as a progressive judge. Roosevelt was probably too hasty in his judgment of Holmes, whose promise developed slowly. The president's instinct was true, but his patience was limited.

ROOSEVELT NOT ONLY MOLDED the modern presidency, he also provided for his successors a model for family life in the White House. The Roosevelts set a joyous and elegant style for living that remained unmatched until the Kennedys came along in 1961.

Any account starts with the matchless First Lady, Edith Kermit Carow Roosevelt, a regally tall, handsome brunette with fair skin and blue eyes, fashionably dressed (her dresses were always American-made), and well read in English and French. She was the most charming and adept First Lady since Dolley Madison of the founding generation. A private person by nature, Edith nevertheless

Edith Kermit Carow Roosevelt,
always well dressed as First Lady

bloomed in the White House with her brilliant social gatherings. She entertained more than any other president's wife before her with dinners, evening gatherings, and lunches. Roosevelt claimed that he spent his entire salary as president, a substantial fifty thousand dollars a year, on social life in the White House. (He did not think a public official ought to make money from his position.) His conviviality was legendary.

Alice Lee Roosevelt, 1902

Edith's role as mother was her prime duty. She suffered two miscarriages in these years, but recovered quickly with little notice. She wanted more children, but Roosevelt thought that six "bunnies" (his term) were enough. Edith was a warm, generous, but stern mother, when necessary, to the Roosevelts' six boisterous children whose antics were

The Roosevelt family in 1903. Left to right: Quentin, the President, Theodore, Jr., Archibald, Alice Lee, Kermit, The First Lady, Ethel Carow

regularly catalogued by a hungry press. There were two girls, Alice and Ethel, although only "Princess" Alice from Roosevelt's first marriage ever made headlines. Mostly, it was Roosevelt's four over-the-top boys—Theodore Roosevelt, Jr., Kermit, Archibald, and Quentin—who interested reporters. They were the youngest boys in the White House since Lincoln's sons. In his day, Tad Lincoln was known for bringing a pet goat into the White House, but a Roosevelt boy did him one better by bringing a pony up the elevator to cheer up a sick brother. The boys went to the famous Groton prep school, and Ted and Kermit went to Harvard.

Roosevelt was known to play cowboys and Indians with his youngest boys, whooping it up in the halls and bedrooms, and they had pillow fights, which scattered feathers all over the rooms. The melees were so spirited that sometimes, when the president was already formally dressed for dinner, he had to change his clothes before going downstairs to his party. Edith was, mostly, a delightful parent, as captured by one little tyke's comment, "When mother was a little girl, she must have been a boy."

Roosevelt's boys adored him, in his many aspects—playing, hunting, hiking, horseback riding, shooting, boating, observing nature. One story about Roosevelt that was both affectionate and manly was that of how the "teddy bear" name came to be. The tale is that while Roosevelt was hunting with a party in Mississippi in 1902, with no success in bagging a much-wanted bear, his friends found a cub and tied it to a tree, ready for shooting. Roosevelt refused the offer as unsporting and let the bear go, with the result that fake baby bears were named Teddy and became an instant and favorite child's toy for generations.

Edith's great contribution to the public life of the country was her 1902 renovation of the White House, which created executive offices for the president's staff of thirty-eight men, the popularly called West Wing. Roosevelt put his assistants and his three secretaries in the new digs, where he also had a large office, thirty feet square, with large windows facing south. He preferred to work out of his study in the White House, however, at a desk sent to him by Queen Victoria. It was made from timbers of the intrepid British ship *Resolute*, which had in 1852 sailed on an expedition in search of the Northwest Passage. Across from it was a fireplace, and over it Roosevelt hung a por-

President Roosevelt, in 1902, in Mississippi,
refusing to shoot a leashed bear cub, which became Teddy Bear

trait of Lincoln. (The first Oval Office for the president was added later, and the more famous, contemporary Oval Office still later.)

The Executive Mansion—it was Roosevelt who renamed it the White House—was renovated under the best architects and designers in the country so that it could be returned to Washington's and Jefferson's classic conception. The nineteenth-century "flub dubs" and "excrescences," as Lincoln called them, were removed, and light from the windows was allowed to enter the beautiful building. From a shabby hotel, once half-home and half-presidential office, the mansion became a little palace, rivaling those in Europe, while retaining its republican character.

Edith was attentive to every detail of the work. The first floor of the new White House consisted of spacious, newly furnished, public rooms, with an enlarged state dining room. The second floor was made entirely private for the first time. There would be no more sharing of the living quarters with strangers traipsing through the rooms on public business. Here, in their private quarters, Edith created a sunny corner bedroom for the president and herself with light, air, and a sense of serenity. It became a Roosevelt favorite because Edith installed some furniture that had been used by the Lincolns. Roosevelt said that he "liked to imagine the Emancipator shambling about . . . his face deeply furrowed and racked in thought."

CHAPTER 7

A Mandate at Last

One must always keep in mind what Abraham Lincoln pointed out—that all of the people can be fooled for part of the time. It may be that this election will come in that part of the time; but it is sure as anything in history can be that the Democrats . . . and their mugwump and capitalistic allies, are playing a bunco game which ought not to take in any but a low order of intelligence.

I am in my own way, a radical democrat myself; that is I am a thorough believer in the genuine democracy of Abraham Lincoln, the democracy of the plain people.

———

The whole Brownsville business had been carried on under my personal supervision; and . . . if there was the slightest doubt on the subject I was exceedingly anxious that everybody concerned should know that I not only accepted but claimed the entire responsibility for the affair.

In the Brownsville case I . . . visited upon Negro soldiers who had been guilty of misconduct the same punishment that I would have inflicted had the offenders been white.

From the information I have, there are probably five or six men who, because of being on pass or being in barracks out of the way, can be legitimately reinstated.

———

I have furnished a safety-valve for the popular unrest and indignation. . . . I am deeply convinced that unless we want to see very violent convulsions in this country, and the certainty of ultimate adoption of State ownership and of very drastic measures against corporations, there must be a steady perseverance in the policy of control over corporations by the Government, which I have advocated.

ROOSEVELT WANTED TO BE PRESIDENT IN his own right. "Of course, I should like to be President, and I feel I could do the work well," he wrote to his friend William Howard Taft in July 1901. To Cabot, a month later, he reported some good news from the West and Southwest after a two-week trip. There are some "genuine popular movements . . . in his behalf." The men who supported Roosevelt were "not nobodies" but various officeholders. He wrote to the journalist William Allen White on August 27 that, if he were nominated, it would be at the "initiative of the people." That is, Roosevelt looked beyond party leaders for a nomination and to high-minded Republicans and "farmers, small businessmen, and upper-class mechanics, who were his natural allies." A few days earlier, he had written to White that he had neither "the temperament, nor the kind of political and moneyed friends to permit of my being put forward by intrigue."

President Theodore Roosevelt, 1903, attached to the world

By the time Roosevelt approached the 1902 off-year elections, he had amassed a record he was proud of and which he believed could propel him toward the Republican nomination for president. He was the most adept chief executive since Lincoln, and he barnstormed the North,

South, and Midwest for the Republican Party. He did not stop for long even after a terrible carriage accident severely injured him in early September. Roosevelt was black-and-blue and his face was swollen. His left shin suffered trauma despite two operations to clean up the infection. Hay estimated that he had avoided death, literally, by two inches. He was amply rewarded for his perseverance. Republicans were returned to office with a thirty-seat majority in the House, and they retained their same majority in the Senate. In his programs, style, ideas, values, and family life, Roosevelt had captivated the nation, energized his supporters, and almost neutralized his Democratic adversaries. It was especially helpful that the Wall Street crowd, especially J. P. Morgan and E. H. Harriman, among others, had favored Roosevelt. The omens were good for Roosevelt as 1904 beckoned. Mark Hanna had been the plutocrats' golden boy for the nomination, but his crown was tarnished as Roosevelt's was burnished. Then Hanna died, unexpectedly, of typhoid fever in 1903.

The sometime Roosevelt friend and jaundiced Henry Adams observed of Roosevelt's obsession to win in 1904, "If you remark to him that God is Great, he asks naively how that will affect his election."

Roosevelt easily won a unanimous Republican nomination for president in June 1904. Surprisingly, he was touted as a writer and a scholar, not a warrior, and he was called the man who most represented the spirit and values of the twentieth century. The Republican Party platform was vague on a revision of the tariff (never a Roosevelt priority, as it would divide the party), labor, the trusts, the Philippines, and foreign policy. Blacks got a nod, as disen-

President Theodore Roosevelt speaking at
Northwestern University, 1903

franchisement was not supported. (Southern states were
engaging in denying the vote to black men.) The most
progressive Republicans were ignored and radicals left
alone. It was a milk-and-water document. There was

nothing of Roosevelt's fiery and explicit calls for action or pledges for the future.

The presidential campaign lacked energy because of the traditional restraints on sitting presidents. They did not go out on the hustings, where Roosevelt was at his best. So Roosevelt wrote letters, instead, to supporters, which were made public. On June 2, he had signaled to Elihu Root, who was engaged in platform writing, how he wanted his party to present itself to the public. Roosevelt listed his accomplishments as president. Among them were prosecuting wrongdoing in the post office; buying the Panama isthmus; settling the coal strike; breaking the Northern Securities Trust; getting a Cuban reciprocity treaty that allowed the importation of sugar to revive its economy; settling the Alaska boundary dispute with England; gaining independence for Cuba; building the navy; reorganizing the army and national guard; irrigating and reforesting the West; reforming the civil service; making high-grade appointments to the federal service with the "same standard for black men and for white, just as for wage-earner and capitalist, for Jew and Gentile, for Catholic and Protestant"; establishing the Department of Commerce and Labor with a bureau of corporations; expanding the Open Door in China; enforcing the Monroe Doctrine regarding Venezuela, with the high court at The Hague as arbiter; and using The Hague for any dispute with Mexico. On another occasion he mentioned continuing to give pensions to veterans and maintaining rural free postal delivery.

There was a yawning gap between what Roosevelt had accomplished and the Republican platform, a gap that did not elude reformist Republicans and gadflies. Nicholas Murray Butler, president of Columbia University, was one such active party member who was disappointed. Roosevelt explained his predicament by comparing himself to Lincoln in a long missive to him on June 3: "Of course I have to compromise now and then; but I have to do astonishing little of it. . . . I have been able to shape my course far more nearly in accordance with the idealistic view than he [Lincoln] was able to shape his." Roosevelt claimed that "all legislation that I cared for was through by the end of the Congressional session." He was a successful president, in his estimation, despite the platform's lack of acknowledgment of his triumphs.

The Democrats ran the conservative Alton B. Parker for president, whom Roosevelt considered "a formidable candidate" because he favored gold currency and had the backing of many wealthy New Yorkers. The spell of William Jennings Bryan over the Democratic Party, with its call for paper money, was broken.

Neither Roosevelt's record nor his progressivism was the main factor in the campaign. Rather, his financial backers provided the fireworks. The chairman of the Republican National Committee, George Cortelyou, was also the secretary of commerce and labor and thus had access to information on corporations, which Democrats had claimed opened the door to blackmail. Roosevelt was incensed by the attack and offered "to appear in the campaign myself, either by speech or letter" to counter the charges, but he was held back. The president did remind his supporters that it was the Justice Department, and not Cortelyou, that enforced antitrust laws.

Roosevelt ordered Cortelyou to return the hundred thousand dollars contributed to the campaign by Standard Oil. He made it clear that there would be no favors to anyone giving money to his campaign. When Parker accused him of blackmailing corporations in October, Roosevelt publicly replied on November 4 that "the statements . . . are atrociously false." Parker had no proof of his assertions.

It wasn't until 1912, in an investigation by the Clapp Committee, that it was revealed that Roosevelt had not known all that was going on. Large corporations had provided more than two million dollars to support his campaign. The treasurer of the Republican Party had ignored the president's injunction. Cortelyou was also deaf to Roosevelt's order. There was "no evidence of blackmail," however, the committee reported, as some major contributors were later caught up in antitrust suits or were adversely affected by the Hepburn Act regulating railroads.

Roosevelt soothed himself in a letter to Cabot during those trying days: "One must keep in mind what Abraham Lincoln pointed out—that all of the people can be fooled for part of the time. It may be that this election will come in that part of the time. . . . The democrats including Parker and their mugwumps [mostly lapsed Republicans] and capitalistic allies are playing a bunco game. . . . Wealthy scoundrels in New York . . . are his [Parker's] great backers."

The president won a second term in a scintillating personal triumph. He exulted to his friend Cabot, "I had no idea that there would be such a sweep." His electoral majority—366 votes—was the greatest up to that time. He won the North and more than 56 percent of the total votes cast. Only the South went Democratic. Now that region was useful to Republicans only during nominating conventions, when blacks, who virtually constituted the southern wing of the party, always voted for the candidates of the party leaders.

Probably the only memorable political quip about Roosevelt's election was uttered, later, by a disgruntled plutocrat, the Pittsburgh steel magnate Henry Clay Frick. He had given the Republican campaign one hundred thousand dollars, most probably after winks by Roosevelt supporters, or on the basis of the bland platform. When Roosevelt continued on his progressive political path, as signaled by his victory statements and, later, in his messages to Congress, Frick commented, "We bought the son of a bitch and then he did not stay bought."

Roosevelt was inaugurated on March 4, 1905. He wore a ring given to him by his admiring secretary of state, John Hay. Inside the ring were strands of Lincoln's hair, cut off the night of the assassination and given to him by Lincoln's son Robert. Hay included a note with the ring that read, "Please wear it to-morrow; you are one of the men who most thoroughly understand and appreciates Lincoln." Hay had, obviously, recalled the letter that Roosevelt had written to him two years before, after receiving Hay's multivolume biography of Lincoln. "I suppose you know Lincoln is my hero," Roosevelt had written. "He was a man of the people who always felt with and for the people, but who had not the slightest touch of the demagogue in him."

The president was elated by the inaugural ceremony, which was a spectacle. It featured the many kinds of plain people he often extolled as his true supporters. It was a colorful, noisy parade, a triumphal march unlike anything that had been seen before or that would be seen again for some time. He exulted in a letter:

I had thirty members of my old regiment as my special guard of honor, riding to and from the Capitol. And in the parade itself, besides the regular army and navy and the national guard, there was every variety of civic organization, including a delegation of coal miners with a banner recalling that I had settled the anthracite coal strike; Porto Ricans and Philippine Scouts; old-style Indians, in their war paint and with horses painted green and blue and red and yellow, with their war bonnets of eagles' feathers and their spears and tomahawks, followed by the new Indians, the students of Hampton and Carlisle, sixty or seventy cowboys; farmers clubs; mechanics clubs—everybody and everything. Many of my old friends with whom I had lived on the ranches and worked in the roundups in the early days came on to see me inaugurated.

Roosevelt at last had his mandate to govern, and it came from those he most earnestly wanted to represent. He confided to the novelist Owen Wister on November 19: "It is a peculiar gratification to me to have owed my election not to the politicians, primarily, not to the financiers . . . but above all to Abraham Lincoln's 'plain people.'" To the historian James Ford Rhodes he wrote ten days later, "I hope I have taken to heart Lincoln's life, at least sufficiently to make me feel that triumph gives less cause for elation than for a solemn realization of the responsibility it entails." He felt most keenly the "towering greatness of Lincoln."

Without hesitation, he spelled out his convictions in two messages to Congress, the first in late 1904 and the second in early 1905. He offered solutions for the many problems he had earlier identified, along with new ones. For starters, and because Washington was a federal city and governed by the Congress, Roosevelt, with help from Jacob Riis, asked for

Sagamore Hill, 1905

legislation to improve the execrable living conditions in the nation's capital. The city was poor and teeming with the wretched sons and daughters of the black freedmen. He asked for slum clearance, the regulation of factory conditions, public parks, and a commission to oversee housing and health for the inhabitants. He sponsored bills for compulsory education, setting up a juvenile court, and regulating employment agencies. He wished to make it a "model city." All his hopes were dashed, and no bills were passed. Then, and now, making the nation's capital a city of light and enlightenment eludes the Congress.

Roosevelt took a giant step toward cleaning up elections at the federal level and curbing corporate venality when, in 1905, he proposed that "contributions by corporations to any political committee or for any political purpose should be forbidden by law." He excluded persons owning or managing corporations from the prohibition. He also asked that public financing for federal candidates through their political parties be instituted—an even more advanced proposition. His suggestions were so astounding that the Tillman Act, an election reform bill, did not pass Congress until 1907. Unfortunately, the act had no enforcement provisions built into it. Still, Roosevelt's goal of curbing corporate money in elections was the beginning of addressing a growing problem over the decades, and until new laws were passed. His acknowledgment of and attempt to limit corporate donations to political parties was a milestone toward making democracy work better.

Roosevelt next tackled the railroad problem. For two years, and before 1904, he had been carefully considering the issue of railroad rebates. Now, emboldened by his election, he felt he could pursue the dodgy practice. He took the occasion of answering a letter from the railroad tycoon Edward Henry (E. H.) Harriman, who actually had written to the president about a different question, to bring up the issue. For years, Harriman had been the poster boy for predatory railroad activities in the West, and reformers and progressives had been railing against him. On November 30, 1904, Roosevelt gave him a heads-up when he said it was "unwise" and "unsafe" not to tackle rebates. Then, in a message to Congress the next month, the president explained why he was addressing this hot issue. Railroads were now at the center of American industrial success, he explained. Roads were the "highways of commerce" and were now clogged with unfair rates and various abuses practiced by trusts. Farmers were injured by the practices, as were small entrepreneurs. These classes of working citizens, the people Roosevelt called his own, were up in arms over the discrimination. He meant to give them justice while also better balancing the economy among groups. He would take on the wealthy railroad men and their allies, the oil men (pipelines were a part of the road problem), and the financiers in the West or on Wall Street.

For months, Roosevelt led, tilted with, and exhorted senators and congressmen of both parties. He even put together informal coalitions on the issue. This was a strategy never used before by Republicans. The Hepburn Act regulating railroads was passed in 1906. It ended the worst abuses practiced by railroad companies. Within a competitive system, the Interstate Commerce Commission henceforth would control rates charged for passengers and freight, on pipelines, at terminals, on refrigeration cars, and on storage facilities. The railroads were also commanded to sell off their steamship lines and coal mines. At last, farmers and small businessmen got some relief from a no-holds-barred economy.

But Roosevelt lost his friends and many other Republicans in the railroad war. Senators Lodge, Spooner, and Knox broke ranks. They were joined by Nelson W. Aldrich and Joseph B. Foraker. When he worked with Democrats in shifting coalitions, even with Ben Tillman of South Carolina, Republican rage was palpable. His actions were a tour de force of presidential power seeking a particular end, regardless of the means. With the Hepburn Act, the federal government would now manage the biggest business in the country. The government's overseeing of such a large sector of the economy was a straight path toward an administrative state, a hallmark of a modern nation in the making. For Roosevelt, it was a signal moment in an emerging pragmatic progressivism.

There was a downside to Roosevelt's railroad victory, however, as the law of unintended consequences kicked in. The largest business interests were beyond fury and, to this day, would just as soon forget Roosevelt's presidency. At the time, big corporations were energized more than ever against him. Complaints poured into the administration. In February 1907 Roosevelt sharply responded to one by the financier Henry Lee Higginson in a letter. He wrote that a study had shown that railroad rates could be lowered 10 percent without affecting profits. In his words, "The present unsatisfactory condition in railroad affairs is due ninety-five percent to the misconduct, the shortsightedness, and the folly of the big railroad men themselves. . . . Not one particle of harm has come to them by federal action."

Another complainer, C. E. Perkins, a former railroad tycoon, wrote to Higginson in late March that administrative decisions made by Roosevelt's regulators regarding railroads were akin to the power possessed by the "Czar of Russia." It was an interesting, if not wholly correct, comparison. Roosevelt's actions were based on law, and not on a supposedly divine power wielded by a head of state. But the extreme comparison showed, if nothing else, the depth of the plutocratic hatred of Roosevelt. The railroad issue simmered all through Roosevelt's presidency.

Roosevelt's war against trusts was broad and went beyond railroads and financial institutions. It included businesses engaged in shoddy practices in providing food and medicines to the American people. He went after the Swift Company beef trust, which allowed appallingly dirty and unsafe conditions in its factories. The nation's meat supply was unsafe. Drugs were also being sold throughout the country that were unhealthful when not outright deadly. Shysters and quacks were in control of so-called medicines. A new group of journalistic reformers, once disparagingly called muckrakers by Roosevelt, were providing searing investigative reports of these dangerous businesses.

Roosevelt grabbed the reins of the struggle, while not allying himself with the first movers, and the Pure Food and Drug Act was passed in 1906. The new law forbade the making, sale, or transporting of adulterated or fraudulently labeled food and drugs sold throughout the country. A Meat Inspection Act enforced sanitary regulation and federal inspection of all plants engaged in interstate commerce. Roosevelt thought the meat, food, and drug bills "noteworthy" in the broad attempt to regulate national corporations dealing with the health and safety of Americans.

Roosevelt called the administering and enforcing of the new regulatory laws the "vital work" of the presidency. He understood the balancing act he was performing in his Square Deal program. He ruminated in 1906, pulling strands from the legacies of the Founding Fathers, that he was a "Jeffersonian" in his "genuine faith in democracy and popular government" and a "Hamiltonian" in the "need for the exercise of broad powers by the national government." The middle class and reformers celebrated his domestic triumphs, as he twined together the two great political legacies of the nation as a foundation.

Roosevelt's whirlwind domestic program included another of his interests—reforming the immigration system. It resulted in the passage of the 1906 Naturalization Act. After years of prodding, from 1903 to 1905, Roosevelt persuaded

A Roosevelt cartoon, 1904

President Roosevelt and Booker T. Washington
at Tuskegee Institute, 1905

Congress to revise the old 1870 law. The Naturalization Act of 1906 created a Bureau of Naturalization within the Department of Commerce and Labor. Roosevelt's aim was to keep out of the country those who were unfit physically, morally, and mentally. Mostly, he wanted better-informed citizens. Under the new law, only immigrants who could read, speak, and understand English could become citizens. Further, in order to ensure proper enforcement, fewer courts were empowered to grant citizenship.

Roosevelt did not want immigration to injure, in any way, the laboring men of the nation, the plain people of his Republican cohort. He never forgot that he was the protector of the "free labor" of Abraham Lincoln's platform. He made his twin goals clear when he wrote to Speaker Cannon, who shepherded all legislation in the House:

> I have two concerns . . . I hope to see such laws enacted as will prevent the administration of immigrants who by their competition tend to lower the standard of living, and therefore the standard of wages of our own laboring men. . . . But in the next and more important place, it seems to me essential from the standpoint of the permanent good of the Republic that we should try only to bring in elements which would be [of] advantage to our community. I do not care what the man's creed or nationality may be, so long as his character is all right and so long as he has the amount of physical and mental fitness that we should be able to demand.

Roosevelt's nod to immigration policy was more tolerant and broad than the stance taken by Congress a generation later, which was more discriminatory and not a little racist, but it was not as liberal as immigration standards of the 1980s.

AFTER HIS ROUGH RIDER EXPLOITS, nothing captured the popular imagination more than Roosevelt's thoroughly innovative, imaginative, and far-reaching program of land usage. Roosevelt became, after Lincoln, the second most important chief executive regarding the use of western lands. Lincoln had signed the Homestead Act, which gave settlers 160 free acres to till. In a new bill, Roosevelt increased the grant to 320 acres; thereby, a million and a half acres were open to settlement by small farmers. "Every acre of agricultural land in every national forest is open for settlement," the president announced. Settlers got free water from irrigation projects, and owners who monopolized water power, but whose watersheds were on federal lands, paid fees to support the land program.

Roosevelt also extended his conservation mandate. He established the Forest Service, and a reforestation program yielded renewable resources. During his presidency, the service protected sixteen million new acres in 150 national forests, quadrupling what already existed. Roosevelt created five national parks, using as a model his beloved Yellowstone Park, established in 1872. Fifty-one wildlife refuges also came into being.

In 1906, Roosevelt signed the Antiquities Act, which gave presidents the executive power to protect wonders of nature that are a part of the nation's heritage. This act is still used in our own time, despite the tumult of developers and the outraged cries of some western congressmen and governors.

Vast acreage was added to conservation; in size, it was almost equal to Jefferson's Louisiana Purchase in 1803. The latter added to the nation's land mass; Roosevelt's conservation program both saved land from despoliation and made some land productive for farmers. And his broad conservation program was a sturdy foundation on which his cousin, the second President Roosevelt, built in the 1930s. Cousin Theodore was able to merge his love of nature and its beauty with his protective instincts, to offer it as a gift to all Americans in perpetuity. Little or, perhaps, nothing else gave him more satisfaction as a public servant.

The two crowded years 1904–6 were not all positive for Roosevelt. In August 1906 in Brownsville, Texas, an event took place that greatly tarred Roosevelt's historical reputation for fairness and equality. One hundred six black soldiers from Fort Brown were accused of killing a white bartender and wounding a police officer in a melee. Their commanding officer's investigation, and two other investigations, found the soldiers guilty. No soldier had been willing to speak to investigators, making the decisions foregone conclusions. Without a trial, Roosevelt summarily dismissed the whole troop from service, even though some were near retirement and six had won the Medal of Honor. Roosevelt's friend Booker T. Washington advised the president that the decision was a grave mistake. Democrats seized the opportunity to attack Roosevelt. Although the Democratic Party was, in general, far more racist than the Republicans, its members gleefully berated Roosevelt and threatened investigations. Roosevelt defended himself by saying that he would have acted the same whether white or black troops were involved. Later, some soldiers were restored to duty.

ROOSEVELT'S MANY LEADERSHIP QUALITIES and intricate program of needs came together in the building of the Panama Canal. He considered the building of the canal his grandest achievement, and his active management of that greatest of enterprises shows why it was successful. Roosevelt tacked from scheme to scheme until he perfected the canal's management. There were complicated and stubborn issues to contend with. From the beginning of the enterprise, malaria was devastating the laborers, and better public hygiene and research for the cause of the disease were needed. Which laborers to employ (contract Jamaican, Chinese, or other) was a contentious issue. (The anti-

Chinese labor issue was as well.) Who should get the private contracts to do the work?

A quick review of the canal's history shows that Roosevelt changed the management of canal work several times until he hit on the perfect solution, that of almost totally centralizing authority. At first he created a decentralized administrative organization for the canal, as provided by Congress. That plan fell almost into chaos by 1904 because the diverse tasks could not be accomplished by uncoordinated managers. Congress refused to act, even after Roosevelt's prodding, so he used his executive power in 1905 to centralize the work more. Still not content with the progress, Roosevelt traveled to Panama (with Edith and others) in 1906. The scientist and efficiency maven needed an on-site inspection. On his return, he once more reorganized the work, giving the administrative authority more responsibility. Roosevelt reorganized the canal's management yet again, in January 1907, with a sleek table of organization for tasks and oversight.

Surprisingly, the reorganization was still insufficient to the task. The building of the canal was the greatest engineering feat ever attempted in modern time. It was no wonder that usual business practices of management faltered. When it became clear to Roosevelt that no private manager was equal to the gigantic task, he turned to the public institution most used to thinking about and doing large tasks—the U.S. Army. The federal government would build the canal, and the brilliant Major General George W. Goethals was put in charge of the work. The army provided centralized, continuous, and undisputed command as well as fine engineers. It also possessed the necessary public relations skills to keep interested parties informed and to

President Roosevelt in Panama, 1906

tamp down all interference. For work that did require contractors, Roosevelt chose experienced businessmen and not politically connected neophytes.

In 1908, an exultant Roosevelt wrote in a letter, "I do not think that any feat of quite such far-reaching importance has been to the credit of the country in recent years; and this I can say absolutely was my own work, and could not have been accomplished save by me or some man of my temperament."

Almost as important as how the canal was built is how it was financed. Roosevelt provided the fifty million dollars necessary from annual surpluses. He did not have to print money—greenbacks—as did Lincoln to pay for the Civil War. (Greenbacks had little gold behind them that business needed to make them a strong currency; farmers preferred untethered, or inflationary, currency.) The surpluses came from the highest tariff ever on imported goods, the Dingley tariff of 1897, which set an average of 57 percent. (It stayed high until 1909 when it was reduced to an average of 38 percent.)

Goethals finished the canal in 1914, on the eve of the Great War. Roosevelt had hoped the war would never come, but he wanted the nation to be prepared for it. The Panama Canal made possible the joining of a two-ocean navy, giving the United States enormous offensive capability in any conflict. In this way, the building of the Panama Canal was not an end in itself but rather a part of Roosevelt's ambitious foreign policy. He was a great strategic planner and was putting together an iron triangle. One side was the canal. Another side was the Monroe Doctrine. The third side was a powerful navy.

Roosevelt worked on increasing the size of the navy throughout his presidency. In early 1907 he explained in a letter, "Our justification for upholding the Monroe Doctrine, and for digging the Panama Canal must rest primarily upon our willingness to build and maintain a first-class fighting fleet." At a later date, he added, "Be it remembered . . . that such a fleet is by far the most potent guaranty of peace which this nation has or can ever have."

Peace through strength was Roosevelt's mantra. It was one of his legacies to a rising nation.

Building a world-class navy was not an easy task. It was expensive, and many suspected that Roosevelt was establishing the means to embark on imperialistic adventures. But he was persistent and eloquent. Year after year, he asked Congress for funds not only to increase the navy's size but also to build the most powerful ships, dreadnoughts that could shoot lighter ships out of the water with their larger guns and from longer distances. He asked, too, for funds to improve the navy's efficiency and to modernize ships. He pored over the size and power of guns on ships and scanned reports of sailors' shooting ability, the size of the ships, the balance within the fleet of different kinds of ships and of each ship's role in a conflict. He compared the navy's ships with those Germany and Japan were building. (Roosevelt did not intend to challenge England's naval supremacy.) Ultimately, he wanted to lay keels for at least four new battleships a year along with new auxiliary ships, such as cruisers, destroyers, and torpedo boats.

Many Republicans and most Democrats were alarmed. Roosevelt's plans were too grandiose and costly. Some self-defined peace Democrats and some progressive Republicans formed a congressional opposition, which challenged a military buildup. They argued against Roosevelt's big navy on the grounds that preparing for war meant going to war. The country was, basically, a pacific, backwater nation. After the horrendous Civil War, it looked inward to recover and to get back to normal endeavors. Farmers still had the greatest representation in the Congress and were uninterested in world affairs except for exporting their crops. The

*President Theodore Roosevelt surveys
the North Atlantic Fleet off Oyster Bay, New York, 1903*

requirements of an industrial economy and an understanding of an emerging imperialist system abroad eluded them. The promise of America was within the country and not abroad. Economic prosperity came from America's farms and factories, and not from colonies.

Roosevelt, sensing a more dangerous world than others, argued to the contrary, that military preparation prevented war. If war came nevertheless, the nation could defend itself: the navy's role would be to carry the offensive against any possible adversary. Democrats, however, wanted a purely defensive navy. They worried that an offensive force would leave the country vulnerable to invasion. Ports would be insecure. To this argument, Roosevelt grandly countered that the army, with its seaside fortifications, was the true defensive force and would protect the homeland. Like so many other Roosevelt initiatives, the naval program and the strategic thinking behind it were ahead of their time.

Despite the strong peace current, Roosevelt won a great victory because Republicans, and some Democrats, were with him. The big-navy chief executive ended up with two new battleships a year, along with other ships of the line, and he was given the tools to modernize the navy. It was enough to build an American navy second only to England's in strength. (It was England's strategy always to keep a navy twice the size of its next competitor.) By 1909, when he left office, Roosevelt could claim that he had authorized the building of half of the active navy ships: 16 of 24 battleships; 6 of 36 cruisers; 12 of 24 submarines; and 16 of 20 destroyers. Most important, Roosevelt built six mighty dreadnought ships to match the English, Germans, and Japanese.

When the country finally entered World War I in 1917, fifty-six ships of 110 had been authorized by Roosevelt. He was truly the father of the modern American navy, as his longtime mentor, Alfred T. Mahan, the eminent naval and strategic authority, always hoped he would be.

Roosevelt was proud of the country's growing naval strength. His only military regret was that he was unable to build up the army as he wished, so fierce was the opposition, mostly by Democrats, against a large standing force. (One can only speculate that the Democrats had long memories of radical Republican reconstruction after the Civil War. Then, military districts were set up to govern the South and to protect the North's victory and the civil rights of the black freedmen. Democrats were not about to enable another such civil takeover.) The president managed, however, to improve the army's administration by introducing the general-staff principle. He also reformed the national guard. Both of these transformations were significant factors in winning World War I.

Despite his naval buildup, Roosevelt was not happy when he learned, through contacts, that England, France, and Germany thought the United States would lose a war with Japan. Japan had bested Russia in 1904–5, and its navy had performed brilliantly. What did America have to match this record? Roosevelt wanted to prove Europe and Japan wrong and to dramatize America's coming of age. He decided to do something that no country had ever attempted. He would send a naval fleet around the world. He had most of the fleet painted a light gray, a color that looked lighter in the sun, and so the soon-to-be famous White Fleet was born.

Roosevelt wanted to impress Japan, which he had watched as a possible adversary for some years, as it militarized itself and looked outward toward the Pacific. That Asian nation had thirteen battleships and eleven armed cruisers. Roosevelt mustered eighteen battleships, eight armored cruisers, six torpedo–boat destroyers, and a few coaling ships for the voyage. More than eighteen thousand sailors were aboard. The White Fleet would test its operative strength, as well as its general efficiency, and would assess the readiness of the nation's coaling stations. In addition, a month of target practice would improve the accuracy of the fleet's guns.

The White Fleet left home waters in December 1907. A recalcitrant Congress was unwilling to provide the money for the shakedown cruise, but Roosevelt thundered that he had enough funds from the military budget to send the fleet out, and it would just remain in foreign waters until money was forthcoming for its return. Congress relented swiftly, outfoxed once more by the master politician in the White House. (The White Fleet's journey ultimately cost about $1.7 million.)

In the course of fourteen months, the ships steamed about forty-six thousand miles around the world with no serious breakdown. The White Fleet was lionized everywhere, including in Japan. It was a brilliant achievement, which captured the popular imagination no less than a later president's landing men on the moon.

When the fleet returned in February 1909, steaming seven miles long into its Virginia port, Roosevelt and dignitaries met it in a proud and wild extravaganza. The homecoming event became the highpoint of Roosevelt's popular acclaim. He was satisfied that he had made his military case: peace required preparedness and the navy would be the cornerstone of American foreign policy in the new century. More than once, Roosevelt had written to doubters, "I never take a step in foreign policy unless I am assured that I shall be able eventually to carry out my will by force." He learned, to his satisfaction, that foreign countries respected American naval strength. Ironically, Japan had given the navy its biggest welcome.

THE YEAR 1907 also had low points. An economic panic scarred the country for months, and plutocrats blamed Roosevelt because of his trust busting. A Mr. Robert Thompson Jr. wrote that "a panic is about to be caused as a result of unreasonable attacks on wealth and business" and added that "if hard times come, they will be due to Rough Rider methods." Thompson had written this to financier Henry Lee Higginson, who passed it on to Roosevelt. The president replied to Higginson on August 12, 1907, that the charges had "a note of lunacy." Roosevelt wrote to another correspondent, "I do not think that what I have done has had any appreciable effect on bringing about the severity of the present situation. . . . The present trouble is worldwide." Roosevelt defined "a condition of 'panic'" to another as "folly raised to the point of craziness" and that "crazy people . . . do not think successfully." To Henry White, on November 27, he opined that "our people do not fully realize the modern interdependence in financial and business relations."

Roosevelt was no financial genius—he always considered his lack of sophistication about finances a great weakness—but he was confident that he knew better than others why the recessionary forces surfaced in March and again in August. As he analyzed it, several years of credit overexpansion and high prices were the result of a remarkable run of prosperity. Then the business cycle turned down with a sharp and unexpected deflation. Other not inconsiderable factors in the money crunch were the need to fund earth-quake reconstruction in San Francisco after the devastating quake of 1906 and the Russo-Japanese War that ended in 1905. The brief panic was really a worldwide phenomenon, with economic forces affecting all major countries tied into the global marketplace. Most historians believe that Roosevelt was basically correct in his assessment: the panic was really a global phenomenon.

The world of boom and bust prevailed. Roosevelt made noises, in letters to concerned Republicans, about what could or could not be done to relieve the shortage of money. He even toyed with an often-discussed notion of creating a federal mechanism that would give the country a flexible currency. He continually tried to calm the markets with public and private statements. But he suggested nothing to Congress, and that body did not act on its own to reform a monetary system that resembled a Rube Goldberg contraption.

Then the crisis became more acute in late October 1907. Some trust–company banks in New York City, the financial center of the nation, began to fail or were threatened by failure. They had not kept enough reserves to satisfy panicked customers. If New York banks failed, they would bring down untold numbers of banks across the country. Roosevelt had no recourse but to turn to the only person who could amass enormous sums of money to rescue the trusts—J. P. Morgan, the most notorious of the robber barons. Morgan virtually bludgeoned New York bankers into pooling their resources to shore up credit by increasing bank reserves. The sum of twenty-five million dollars was raised, and Roosevelt put up an equal amount of money in

U.S. Treasury funds. Roosevelt also ordered the issuance of government bonds that buyers could use for a variety of stabilizing efforts. The credit market returned to an even keel, and mostly only speculators, for whom no sensible American shed tears, were hurt. The economy soon returned to high prosperity until the Great War, the only exception being 1911.

ROOSEVELT ALSO FACED a small crisis in 1907 over the care of veterans. These former soldiers, aided and abetted by the corrupt and insatiable Grand Army of the Republic lobby, bombarded Congress with thousands of individual petitions for pensions. Then, in 1907, Congress passed the extraordinary McCumber Act, which gave monthly pensions to all veterans of the Mexican and Civil wars who had served ninety days or more. Old soldiers no longer needed to be disabled to claim a pension. Now the government would send monthly pension checks to all: $12 to men 62 years old; $15 at age 65; and $70 at age 75. The McCumber Act had created a welfare state for veterans. It would cost fifty million dollars a year.

By executive authority, Roosevelt had raised pension benefits for veterans in 1904. At the time, he expressed his concern to the chairman of the congressional committee on pensions. He worried that the country was "approaching the danger line in this class of legislation. . . . Instead of taking up cases of exceptional merit, we are now really simply granting favors to great multitudes of people." It was not a "healthy" thing to do. It "discriminates against men as worthy as those who get the pensions." Of course, the McCumber Act made things worse for someone holding this view.

Overall, Roosevelt's domestic record was progressive and ample. It is true that the superrich saw him, in his words, as a "wild-eyed revolutionist." This baffled him, as he viewed himself as always being engaged in balancing capital and labor, with the federal government standing above both as an honest broker. In an engaging letter to his English friend and diplomat, Cecil Spring Rice, Roosevelt characterized his role and put it in comparative, historical perspective: "Here at home I am engaged in the pleasing task of trying to prevent the plutocracy on the one hand and the anarchistic labor group on the other from traveling exactly the same path that in Russia have made the autocracy and the wild-eyed radicals almost equally impossible, almost equally dangerous to the future of the country."

Toward the end of his term, Roosevelt wrote to various supporters that "the super-rich opposed him because they no longer ran the national government." Now they had "to reckon with the federal government" because of all the regulatory bills passed. "The owners of predatory wealth hate me . . . [and] they have no moral scruples of any kind whatsoever." It infuriated him that they not only acted against him but supported the Democratic Party. He considered the Democrats corrupt, reactionary, and racist. Over and over, he reminded all that "his" Republican Party was that of the middling classes, on the land and in the factories; that is, of all the men who sought equality and opportunity.

At the end of his presidency, Roosevelt mellowed a bit in his estimate of Congress. He declared that no recent Congress had done as much good work for the nation. In his experience, he recorded, it was the best ever in responding to the needs of society. Speaker Cannon, however, the cool recipient of Roosevelt's legislative torrent (he may have been the first president to draft bills for the Congress, depriving it, often, of its first-mover role), commented wryly, "Roosevelt's all right, but he's got no more use for the Constitution than a tomcat has for a marriage license."

CHAPTER 8

The Imperial Years

I am trying to make tropical American peoples understand that on the one hand they must behave themselves
reasonable well, and that on the other I have not the slightest intention of doing anything that is not for their own
good. . . . I like the Russian people, but I abhor the Russian
system of government, and I cannot trust the word of those
at the head. The Japanese I am inclined to welcome as a
valuable factor in the civilization of the future . . . [but] they
distrust . . . the white race. They feel puffed up over their
strength. . . . [The Kaiser] is altogether too jumpy, too
volatile in his policies . . . for me to feel he is in any way such
a man as for instance Taft or Root. . . . My business is to
look primarily after the interests of my own country. . . . We
have a pretty good navy with which to fight [in 1905]. I shall
hope that . . . I can keep the respect not of Berlin, but of St.
Petersburg and Tokyo both. . . . I shall hope to keep on good
terms to all.

I do not at all like the social conditions at present. The
dull, purblind folly of the very rich men; their greed and arrogance, and the way in which they have unduly prospered

by the help of the ablest lawyers, and too often through the weakness or shortsightedness of the judges or by their unfortunate possession of meticulous minds; these facts, and the corruption in business and politics, have tended to produce a very unhealthy condition of excitement and irritation in the popular mind.

———

[Re] the trouble we are having in connection with the Japanese in California. . . . Under the lead of the trades unions the San Francisco people . . . have been indulging in boycotts against Japanese restaurants; have excluded the Japanese children from the public schools, and have in other ways threatened, sometimes by law and sometimes by the action of mobs, the rights secured to Japanese in this country by our solemn treaty arrangements with Japan. I am doing everything in my power to secure the righting of these wrongs . . . thru the Department of Justice . . . sending . . . out to California . . . communicating with the Governor of California. . . . It is possible I may have to use the army in connection with boycotting or the suppression of mob violence.

IN THE NINETEENTH CENTURY, AMERICAN presidents had bought foreign lands at the edges of the country that stretched the nation outward while keeping it within the boundaries of the North American continent. William McKinley, however, had conquered Spanish colonies and had gained the Philippines, Samoa, and Puerto Rico, which were not contiguous with the United States. He defended his seizures as a mission of civilizing backward peoples—a transparent delusion since the Philippines, for example, had been Christianized for hundreds of years by the Catholic Church—but he satisfied Republicans. With his extraordinary decisions, the brave Civil War soldier turned chief executive became the first imperial president.

Roosevelt approved of McKinley's actions, and he appropriated the imperial mantle when he himself became president. The crucial question confronting him was: What should be done in a world that had become unstable, and possibly dangerous to the United States, now that it stretched beyond its continental boundaries and the vast waters of the Atlantic and Pacific oceans were no longer natural protectors?

Roosevelt understood that the earth was shifting under his feet. He now had colonies to protect from imperialminded Europeans and a new Japan. He needed a worldview and a strategy for the new age. Roosevelt sought to maintain outwardly friendly relations with a bumptious Germany, even as he harbored private suspicions about its intentions under Emperor William II. When England decided to reach out to Japan in 1902 with a treaty that was subsequently renewed, Roosevelt became even more mindful of the Japanese nation. England's intent was to protect its interests in the Far East and, especially, in India because Russia had been coveting it. To secure this exotic land, the jewel in its imperial crown, England thought it best to ally with Japan, Russia's adversary. In Roosevelt's keen observation, England's new geostrategic action made the Pacific safe for others, like the United States, as its naval power had once made the Caribbean an American lake in the nineteenth century. It seemed natural to Roosevelt, therefore, that England would want warmer relations with the United States.

What did Europe and Asia think of the new American president, who was a keen politician, brave soldier, and reformer? The great world powers saw an intelligent, strong, honorable, engaged, and ambitious leader. His seemingly aristocratic background worked in his favor, too. The greatest European countries—Germany, England, Russia—were monarchical and grandly class conscious. (France's snobbishness was based on past glory rather than a royal system.) Not a few of the highborn leaders and opinion makers of England, Germany, and Japan, who were in touch with Roosevelt over the years, were old acquaintances, or were even Harvard men he knew. A contemporary at Harvard, for example, was the Japanese diplomat Baron Kentaro Kaneko, who was stationed in Washington. Roosevelt's rising reputation made him an attractive person to help the great powers negotiate a peaceful settlement to one war and to disentangle other disputes. These were firsts for the United States.

When the earliest serious challenge to the status quo in the new century occurred with the Russo-Japanese War of 1904–5, Roosevelt was sought as a peacemaker. Yet, he did not quickly agree to pleas for help. Did he want to play in the balance-of-power game of European nations? Privately, and separately, he had advised both Russia and Japan to make peace, as he turned away the several feints from both countries to get involved. Then Japan, secretly and urgently, asked him to help end the war it had started with Russia. It seemed a propitious moment, and Roosevelt signaled his willingness to be a peacemaker. As Roosevelt put it, "I took the position I finally did not of my own volition but because events so shaped themselves that

I would have felt as if I was flinching from a plain duty if I had acted otherwise."

Roosevelt's negotiations in ending the Russo-Japanese War were both masterly and a personal triumph. He intuited that peace could only be made by "disregarding the old conventional diplomatic methods." Having a head of state as neutral arbiter was new. He wanted Japan to realize the fruit of its stunning military victory, but he did not want Russia to be so beggared as to make it a cipher in world politics. That would especially unbalance power in Europe, which had been stabilized since 1815 at the Congress of Vienna, which put Europe back together after Napoleon had ravaged it. Roosevelt was outwardly impartial, and he treated both sides equally in the social and diplomatic arrangements of the peacemaking process. He strenuously avoided playing favorites, though both of the warring parties feared he would. Two instances show his skill. When the diplomats met on the presidential yacht, the *Mayflower*, before they headed for Portsmouth, New Hampshire, for negotiations, Roosevelt made his toast not at a formal dining table, where one country would be at his right and favored, but while everyone stood. Then he arranged a buffet meal, and all sat at a round table. In these ways, all of the nations' representatives shared his company, and no one took pride of place. He chatted in fractured French to all, and his bonhomie put the negotiators at ease and in a peacemaking frame of mind.

In the treaty, Japan got half of Sakhalin Island for winning the war—Russia kept the other half—and an effective suzerainty over Korea. It did not get the indemnity from Russia it had badly wanted. Roosevelt convinced Japan that going back to war, even for a month to secure an indemnity, would eat up the money and would thus be a futile gain. Japan was quietly unhappy with the treaty, but outwardly bowed to it. A weakened Russia turned inward, and the czar brutally put down a revolution in 1905 meant to depose him.

Germany required special attention in European power politics, not only because it had become the strongest nation on the continent, but also because William II was seemingly unstable. Roosevelt was not unaware that the new Germany was smarting at being left out of the newly forming world order. The kaiser needed watching. Sure enough, in 1905, William precipitated a new brouhaha requiring Europe's attention and, soon, Roosevelt's as well. The kaiser coveted the exotic land of Morocco on the northwest coast of Africa, which had staggered into the new century under a rather despotic and chaotic king, who allowed a porous Open Door policy. The year before, an Anglo-French entente effectively looked to France's becoming the protector of Morocco. In exchange, France would not covet Egypt, where England held sway. Italy and Spain seemed ready to accept the grand bargain, but Germany was not. Clearly, Morocco was not a plum ripe for picking, but the kaiser reached for it anyway. He proclaimed support for the independence of Morocco as he steamed into Tangier on one of his impressive vessels.

The kaiser rattled his saber and haughtily demanded an international conference to discuss the equal rights of nations in Morocco. The English and French resented his interference in their cozy Moroccan sphere, but when the kaiser asked Roosevelt to be an honest broker to arrange a settlement, it made a conference inevitable, and England and France grumpily acceded.

At first, Roosevelt was dubious about entering the fray. He was busy with his domestic program, and the United States had no stake at all in the Moroccan contretemps. In his inimitable language, the American chief said to Taft, "We have no fish to fry." Later, he changed his mind. In a replay of the secret kind of negotiation he had been so successful with in his recent Russo-Japanese mediation, Roosevelt got France to agree to a meeting and Germany to pledge to follow the U.S. lead. The powers met at Algeciras in southern Spain in 1906 and, in effect, gave France control over Morocco. William felt cheated but, hoist on his own petard, agreed to Roosevelt's deal.

Roosevelt's diplomatic victory came at a great cost, however. It reinforced the kaiser's fear of encirclement by France and Russia, and it put an end to "his [the kaiser's] desire to be friendly with England." (He expressed both sentiments in private letters to Roosevelt, whom he considered "a gentleman" who would keep his secrets.) The disgruntled kaiser also began a vast program of building naval dreadnoughts so that Germany could challenge the supremacy of the English navy, which had begun building these weapons of great destruction.

Roosevelt received many kudos at home and abroad for his diplomatic triumphs, and they were capped off in 1906 when he was awarded the Nobel Peace Prize. He was the first American to win a Nobel in any field. (It took almost a hundred years for another American president, Jimmy Carter, to be so honored in 2002.) Roosevelt did not pocket the award, forty thousand dollars, but set up an industrial peace committee in Washington, for he thought "in modern life, it is as important to work for the cause of just and righteous peace in the industrial world as in the world of nations."

Roosevelt stretched the power of the chief executive in foreign affairs, as he had in the domestic domain. It was in foreign policy, however, that he propelled the country into the modern world most notably. An early instance was his China policy. McKinley had ventured into China when he enunciated the Open Door in 1899, a policy that American merchants, who had once gotten rich in the China trade, wanted. As European countries became more aggressive in carving out cities and areas of China as exclusive enclaves for their businessmen, McKinley and American commercial interests sought to open up trade for all. American commercial interests, at the time, were negligible compared with other powers' investments, but American merchants and industrialists looked to better times—for example, to possibly building Chinese railroads.

Roosevelt's continuation of McKinley's Open Door, but with a new emphasis on naval power at the ready, led to unfortunate results. Within a generation, trade behind guns turned into gunboat diplomacy. Force, not negotiation, characterized the protection of the national interest. This is not to say that the Europeans in China were not armed. They also maintained force to protect their interests, and their military presence was hated the most.

Roosevelt's unfortunate China policy was reinforced by his low opinion of the Chinese laboring class. And it was this blinkered view that affected Chinese immigration to the United States. For example, by his direct order in mid-June 1905, under U.S. laws and the so-called spirit of its treaties, Roosevelt ordered that "all Chinese of the coolie" class, that is, of the laboring class, were "absolutely prohibited" from coming into the country. This he tempered by stating that "the widest and heartiest courtesy toward all merchants, teachers, students, and travelers," as well as "officials" or "representatives" of the Chinese government could "come and go of their own free will." The president warned American officials that they were to apply this order without "harshness" or "discourtesy" or "inconvenience" or "annoyance," and any variance from it would "be cause for immediate dismissal." He tried to put balm in his order, but it was a racist policy.

Roosevelt's anti-Chinese immigration order was a result, also, of an important preoccupation in his domestic program with the protection of the American workingman against unfair competition. As well, his Chinese immigration policy seemed a practical solution to the difficult dilemma of how to deal with another class of racial hatreds that Americans harbored, especially in California. In 1902, the Chinese Exclusion Act had been passed by Congress, following others that had expired, to prohibit the immigration of Chinese laborers. The nation was already scarred by white hatred of the children and grandchildren of the freedmen. Southerners were subjecting blacks to illegal forms of segregation and the crime of lynching. Roosevelt could and did expose what was happening in the South. He now hoped to keep the West from similar racial hatreds against Chinese immigrants. He wanted to prevent racial and labor wars. He didn't challenge the new, illiberal Exclusion Act, but he would not stand for vigilante violence against Chinese residents.

Roosevelt took a different view of Japanese immigrants. Unlike China, Japan had become educated and Westernized in the late nineteenth century, and it had won a great victory over Russia in 1905. Self-important in the Pacific, the Japanese were not to be trifled with in world affairs. Japanese immigrants were to be treated well in America.

In 1905, Roosevelt's policy toward the Japanese came under direct challenge when the California legislature passed an outrageous resolution calling Japanese "coolies" "immoral, intemperate, quarrelsome men bound to labor for a pittance." Emboldened by this act of folly, the San Francisco School Board announced in 1906 that it would segregate Japanese immigrants in its public schools. The proud Japanese government raised a diplomatic furor in Washington over the school issue, causing a crisis in Japanese-American relations. Roosevelt was furious with the Californians. He referred to them as "infernal fools" in a private letter, and he wrote to the governor of California expressing his concern over "the foolish and wanton insult to Japan." Roosevelt said he was "absolutely opposed to any discriminatory legislation." He raged that this was no time to insult the Japanese, as it would upset a delicate diplomatic balance between the two countries and put American territories in the Pacific in jeopardy. San Francisco's racist policy was "a wicked absurdity."

In looking into the situation more deeply, Roosevelt learned that Californians were really afraid of the influx of Japanese "coolies," because they were taking American jobs for lower pay. California legislators wanted to stop Japanese immigration, as they had stopped the influx of Chinese "coolies" in the Exclusion Act of 1885, which was renewed in 1904. Japan had voluntarily limited emigration to the

United States after 1900, yet the number of emigrating laborers had greatly increased. Americans in San Francisco were genuinely concerned about the Japanese presence in their schools because among the ninety Japanese students in the schools were several adults whom they thought unsuited to mingle with children But for the most part, the public schools had become surrogates for San Franciscans' real fears about losing jobs.

Roosevelt worked to change San Francisco's school policy. He invited the school board to the White House to discuss the issue, and he wrote friendly diplomatic notes to the Japanese government and to his Japanese acquaintances with diplomatic contacts. The president acted to tamp down racism and to prevent any possible mob violence. He even made preparations to use the army to protect Japanese immigrants from vigilante attacks in San Francisco.

Later, in 1906 the San Francisco School Board revised its policy to allow foreign students to attend the public schools, provided that they knew English and were of the appropriate age. The schools were thus legally desegregated. As things worked out, however, the school board segregated all foreign students from Asia because it found them neither age-appropriate nor bilingual: ninety-three persons, including Korean, Japanese, and Chinese, were thus banned from San Francisco schools. Roosevelt had achieved a pyrrhic victory in his quest for racial toleration, but at least he had avoided a diplomatic crisis. In 1907, San Franciscans once more rioted against the Japanese. Then things simmered down after Roosevelt offered Japan a gentleman's agreement, which would limit the immigration of Japanese workers to the United States (students and professionals were exempt from the quotas).

A troubled Roosevelt ruminated to his old Harvard acquaintance on the issues of the differences between peoples and the hair-trigger temper of Americans on immigration questions. He wrote in 1907:

> My dear Baron Kaneko: Nothing during my Presidency has given me more concern than these troubles. . . . A marvelous progress has been made in the relations of Japan with the Occidental nations. . . . Now gentlemen, all educated people, members of professions, and the like, get on so well together. . . . But the half century has been too short a time for the advance to include the laboring classes of the two countries.

Another generation would be needed, Roosevelt continued, for the acceptance of Japanese laborers in America. Meantime, "the best thing to do was to prevent the laboring classes . . . from going in any numbers to the other." (American laborers were not welcome in Japan.) He reminded the baron that the "business of statesmen is to try constantly to keep international relations better, to do away with the causes of friction, and to secure as nearly ideal justice as actual conditions permit." In 1908, Japan responded, positively, to the gentleman's agreement that would restrict Japanese immigration. Perhaps the appearance in a Japanese harbor of the powerful White Fleet showed that the United States was acting from strength, not fear, in proffering the agreement.

A SNAPSHOT OF THE UNITED STATES in 1906 would show that the educated elite was progressive and favorable toward Roosevelt. The Republican Congress, however, was getting more conservative in its attitude toward reform, although later that year, in November, Republicans held onto both houses of Congress. Roosevelt happily wrote to Taft on November 18: "We have won all along the line and everything is as satisfactory as possible."

The canny Roosevelt knew that progressivism now resided more in the presidency than in the Congress. He still intended to expand it and to bring the Congress along. As a result, the last two years of Roosevelt's presidency would prove to be the most remarkable of all in his demands, and his rhetoric was never more insistent or powerful. Roosevelt went on the attack against known evils and their enablers. The *Wall Street Journal* succinctly caught Roosevelt's last hurrah as president when it observed in January 1907 that he was once more fighting "gross and corrupting extravagance, the misuse of swollen fortunes, the indifference to law, the growth of graft, the abuses of great corporate power."

Roosevelt himself characterized the continuing political battle in a letter:

> The policies for which I stand have come to stay. Not only will I not change them, but in their essence they will not be changed by any man that comes after me, unless the reactionaries should have their way. . . . I am amused by the shortsighted folly of the very wealthy men and . . . how large a proportion of them stand for what is fundamentally corrupt and dishonest. Every year that I have lived has made me a firmer believer in the plain people—in the men who gave Abraham Lincoln his strength—and has made me feel the distrust of the over educated dilettante type and, above all of . . . the plutocratic type.

On April 29, 1907, Roosevelt wrote to Republican Governor Albert Baird Cummins of Iowa about "the present crisis of the Republican party," and his role in it:

> [We cannot] submit to the domination in the Republican party of those selfish interests which have long felt that the Government was simply an instrument to further their ends. . . . The struggle should not be over men, but over policies and principles. . . . [Republicans should be] zealously devoted to the great progressive and reforming movement to which . . . the Republican party is now . . . committed in the nation at large.

In August, even though the nation was reeling from a panic over money, Roosevelt attacked the very rich by calling them "malefactors of great wealth," thereby also coining one of the most colorful phrases of his presidency. His attacks startled the conservative business community once more within his party while riling up the populist element, the most left-leaning cohort, among the progressives.

Then, in his annual message in December, Roosevelt asked for the national incorporation of businesses and the regulation of interstate corporations. Individual states, he argued, had been unable to regulate corporations in interstate commerce. He also demanded an inheritance and an income tax. Once more, he suggested putting railroads on an honest basis to avoid hurtful speculation in their stock and to protect agricultural shippers. He would do this by regulating the sale of securities floated by railroads and by basing rates charged to customers on a physical evaluation of the properties and not on phantom assessments.

Roosevelt's attempt to tax the very rich, both to keep them from becoming a powerful, moneyed aristocracy and from passing on immense wealth that could create almost royal dynasties, more than outraged the wealthy classes. They fought such taxes then, would fight them for a generation, and would make the protection of wealth a cornerstone of Republicanism after his presidency.

In the same message, Roosevelt also called for an eight-hour day for laborers—at the time, twelve- and fourteen-hour days, six days a week, were not uncommon—and for workingman's compensation, as injured workers who lost their jobs were cast into poverty. He also requested a limit on the use of court injunctions that forbade strikes, which were blows against labor unions. These court actions were commonly used at the time, and Roosevelt thought they ought to be replaced by the compulsory investigation of large labor conflicts. Wherever and whenever he reasonably could, Roosevelt wanted to elevate labor to a more equal footing with capital.

Relentlessly, Roosevelt lobbied Republicans to protect the working and middling classes, which he thought were the important parts of his revered party of Lincoln. He disliked what seemed to be evolving around him, which was a party of superrich men allied to pensioners, most of them from the Civil War, who were more than ever beholden to the Republicans. Roosevelt was on fire in his last White House crusade in 1907 and 1908 to tame capitalism, to purify politics and the courts, and to make citizens moral.

The president became more and more active in his demands. At the end of January 1908, another presidential message landed on congressional desks, this one even more radical than the last. Roosevelt not only reminded the Congress of his December 1907 proposals, but he now also asked for a new law to regulate the stock market, which he considered a form of gambling. He wanted the buying of stocks to be as safe as putting money in a bank—banks being state regulated, at least. Then, to these hot-button demands, he added yet another new one: he wanted state courts curbed. They had for too long favored large corporations and trusts at the expense of labor in disputes.

But the Congress was dubious about his radical suggestions. By late 1907, after Roosevelt stabilized the panic-stricken economy, the Congress was unwilling to upset big business, the rich, and conservatives, or the old ways of doing things. Roosevelt had badly lacerated the laissez-faire governmental engine, but it had not died. Congress would not engage in any more reforms despite progressive rumblings from reformers, farmers, and industrial laborers. These classes were joined in their bootless quests with many educated intellectuals who were following the building of welfare states abroad. A few of them were even reading Marx.

The last year of Roosevelt's eventful presidency was marked by bitter legislative antagonism and even an attempt to censure the president. Then there was the reactionary work of the courts. There were reversals of major antitrust decisions as well as the striking down of social legislation—workers' compensation, for example. (Employers would no longer be responsible for worker injuries.) All these retrogressive actions fired up counterattacks by Roosevelt against congressional inaction and the courts for their using "legal fictions" to invalidate laws.

Roosevelt, undeterred by attempts to clip his wings and operating under executive discretion, kept up the battle. He wanted the progressive wing of the Republicans to dominate the party and carry forward for a generation.

The President and First Lady, 1908

These progressives would not be the wealthy class. They were the common men who worked for a living and were entrepreneurial. He wanted progressives who were reformers to govern. Their strength was that they acknowledged problems and worked to solve them. He offered his active leadership as the model for a Republican president. The chief executive must have a proven character and must be imbued with the notion that he has obligations to the rich and the poor (an 1899 Roosevelt statement). He must balance class interests, respect and protect all races and creeds, protect the nation's natural bounty, keep the nation defended through strength, and take his place in the world as a respected leader and peacemaker.

As Roosevelt's presidency wound down, opinion makers were at work assessing his foreign and domestic policies. Democrats charged him with being militaristic and interventionist (charges that still find their way into modern biographies). Roosevelt always defended his armament programs and forward military actions as preventive. He believed "foreign policy was sustained by a force in being, as well as by good intentions." His guide was "never to draw unless you mean to shoot." His record shows that, over and over again, in response to European imperial actions, he chose negotiation and order over conflict. He kept his major interventions within the Caribbean basin, always trying to convince the American people that it was in their national interest to keep countries democratic and stable. A prime concern was Cuba, whose fledgling democracy seemed always in peril. Its 1903 constitution allowed the United States to intervene; only reluctantly did Roosevelt invade the island in 1906 when its corrupt government became unstable and violence broke out. (The troops left in 1909.) That year he also sent troops to two other small Caribbean countries, Santo Domingo and Honduras, to stabilize them and protect life and property. A true military leader would probably have tried to conquer these nations and attach them to the United States. Roosevelt never contemplated taking new lands after the Spanish-American War acquisitions.

Roosevelt also eschewed militarism when he became interested in international arbitration treaties and naval disarmament. Over the years, he had submitted arbitration treaties that gave the president the powers to initiate arbitration on his own. The Senate rejected them and did not approve this initiative until after his presidency, and only if it was consulted first. Roosevelt believed that the chief executive needed independence in dealing with foreign powers and that the legislature was ill suited for such a task. And he was willing to establish precedents for his successors to follow. There was a meeting on arbitration issues, but this First Hague Conference failed.

European powers, heedful only of their own needs in their smoldering cockpit, pressed ahead in their attempts to avoid war and called for a Second Hague Conference. It met in 1907, and Roosevelt was most interested in the agenda item on naval disarmament. He calculated that it would be to his country's advantage to freeze naval shipbuilding to keep the militaristic Japanese as the fifth naval power, with England first and America second. But all the grand ideas for peace and for keeping, or for restoring, the balance of power found little support. The second conference also failed.

Roosevelt's inventiveness in governing continued to the last. He added to his legacy on the environment by proposing a regional combination to protect nature. He called a conference of governors to discuss common action. The states, combining regionally, could do as much as a federal law could accomplish to protect the nation's natural resources. It was a new blueprint for future environmental initiatives. Regionalism was born in the progressive wing of the Republican Party. The call for action was so ahead of its time, however, that the actual event accomplished little that was tangible.

During his final year in office, Roosevelt's first priority was finding a suitable successor. He pinned his hopes for protecting his progressive policies on selecting a mirror image of himself. He settled on Taft of Ohio, but he had to row with muffled oars for months because conservatives might not accept a Roosevelt hand-picked successor and because western progressives liked the attractive Robert La Follette of Wisconsin. Roosevelt told Taft in the summer of 1907 that he wanted him to be president. Taft had a stellar record as a jurist in state and federal courts, and he was a trusted Roosevelt aide. He had held the post of governor general of the Philippines, and he had also been a negotiator in troubles in Cuba, Panama, and Puerto Rico, as well as in disagreements with Japan, prior to joining the cabinet as secretary of war. An almost perfect number two man, he was now being readied to be number one; historically, this was often an impossible and heartbreaking rise in politics. (The sitting vice president, Charles W. Fairbanks of Indiana, was never considered by Roosevelt.)

In his person, Taft was genial and relaxed. He had a conventional mind that was light-years away from Roosevelt's originality. He also lacked Roosevelt's focus and his mind-boggling vitality and zest for politics. Taft had a totally juridical demeanor that was now being stuffed into a highly charged political office called the Roosevelt presidency. He was progressive in politics only when in the presence of Roosevelt's blinding light. In Roosevelt's dark absence, Taft was a cautious man inside the progressive web.

On July 30, 1907, Roosevelt made his choice public (it had already been leaked) when he wrote to the influential western journalist William Allen White: "Taft comes nearer than anyone else to being just the man who ought to be President. . . . Taft, in point of courage, sagacity, inflexible uprightness and disinterestedness, wide acquaintance with fundamental problems, seems to me to stand above any other man."

At the Republican convention in June 1908, Taft easily won the nomination on the first ballot, after the conventioneers gave a forty-nine-minute tribute to Roosevelt that almost stampeded the convention toward him. The platform was bland, however, and the campaign was lackluster. Roosevelt was unable to get Taft to muster the energy to make campaign-like visits, give interesting talks, or write stirring public letters. Still, Taft won the presidency against William Jennings Bryan with a margin that was about half of Roosevelt's four years before. And Republicans retained control over both houses of Congress. Roosevelt was genuinely pleased. He was confident that progressivism within the Republican Party was safe in his friend's hands.

On leaving the White House, Roosevelt was a young and vigorous man. Characteristically blunt, he wrote, "I have done my work; I am perfectly content." But what would he now do? For a moment, friends thought he might make a good president of Harvard, as he had been an overseer of that not-yet grand institution since 1895. Then there were those who suggested the possibility of his becoming mayor of New York, a senator, or even a congressman like the redoubtable John Quincy Adams, whose bright later years put in shadow a failed presidency. But

Roosevelt was a triumphal president, and he did not need to prove himself anymore. Someone quipped that he ought to be made bishop, probably the only suggestion most suited to Roosevelt's august role at the end of his presidency. But he made his own plans, and even if he broke Edith's heart in doing so, he was off to Africa, where he would be hunting truly big game.

CHAPTER 9

Too Much Fame

Our hunting trip lasted three weeks. . . . I have killed four lions and two small ones, a bull rhino (which charged viciously, and might have done mischief had it not been for a lucky rather than a skillful shot which dropped him at fourteen paces), two giraffes, a zebra and various kinds of antelopes. . . . I have shot neither well or badly . . . but have killed most of the things that I especially desired to kill—the lions and rhino.

————

The Taft people have been wild that I should come out in a flaming general endorsement of the Taft Administration, which would be bitterly resented by most of my staunchest friends. The greatest service I can render to Taft . . . is to try to help the Republican Party to win at the polls this Fall [1910], and that is what I am trying to do. . . . I have been in a position of inconceivable difficulty. . . . It is my personal interest that Taft should succeed himself; and all that I can consciously to effect this will be done. . . . It is not often that one is able to be thoroughly satisfied; and when we cannot do the best, then, as Abraham Lincoln said, "we have to do the best possible."

We Progressives hold that the words of the Declaration of Independence, as given effect by Washington and as construed and applied by Lincoln, are to be accepted as real, and not as empty phrases. We believe that in very truth this is a government by the people themselves, that the Constitution is theirs, that the courts are theirs, that all the governmental agents and agencies are theirs. . . . It is for the people themselves finally to decide all questions of public policy and to have their decision made effective. . . . Our platform is a covenant with the people of the United States. . . . We Progressives are trying to represent what we know to be the highest ideals and the deepest and most intimate convictions of the plain men and women. . . . We here, in America, hold in our hands the hope of the world.

NO ONE COULD HAVE PREDICTED THAT Roosevelt would have so eventful a time and so short a life after his presidency. Not yet fifty-two years old when he left the White House, he was still full of vigor. At first he needed to get out of the spotlight; afterward, to have opportunities fully to engage himself. A literary career would not satisfy this titan of the new century. What else was there? Numerous possibilities for every kind of activity opened up to interest him. The last decade of his life was momentous in the Roosevelt saga that was also a national, and often an international, story.

Clad in his Rough Rider coat and accompanied by a band playing "There'll Be a Hot Time in the Old Town Tonight," Roosevelt sailed on March 23, 1909, first on the *Hamburg* from New York to Naples and then on the *Admi-*

ral to East Africa. He packed nine pairs of glasses and a contract worth fifty thousand dollars to write about his adventures. The book he wrote, *African Game Trails*, which eventuated from his articles, was published in 1910 in two volumes. Traveling with him was his son Kermit, three naturalists from the Smithsonian, a surgeon, and friends. He also carried a small library of books. It was the largest and best-equipped scientific safari ever to enter East Africa and probably the most expensive as well. Roosevelt's philanthropist friends underwrote the enterprise. Andrew Carnegie gave thirty thousand dollars. Roosevelt himself paid for his family's costs of twenty thousand.

For the first part of the trip, out from Mombassa on the Uganda railroad, the excited hunter rode in a high, jerry-built seat over the cowcatcher of the engine pulling his train through a game area. By now Roosevelt was blind in one eye, and the other was not up to par. "It was literally like passing through a vast zoological garden," he said.

The group then made a safari to enter the jungle. Roosevelt recorded that "our preparations were necessarily on a very large scale; and as we drew up at the station the array of porters [two hundred various helpers] and of tents looked as if some small military expedition was about to start. The provisions carried were the normal ones." He added "Boston baked beans, California peaches, and tomatoes," presumably in cans.

What did the great hunter look like? In his words, "While hunting I wore heavy shoes, with hobnails or rubber soles; khaki trousers, the knees faced with leather, and the legs buttoning tight from the knee to below the ankle, to avoid the need of leggings; a khaki-colored army shirt; and a sun-helmet, which I wore in deference to local advice, instead of my beloved and far more convenient slouch-hat. My rifles were an army Springfield 30-caliber, stocked and sighted to suit myself; a Winchester 405; and a double-barrelled 500–450 Holland, a beautiful weapon presented to me by some English friends." (The last was called a double elephant rifle.)

The expedition was an enormous success scientifically, but it went mostly unpublicized because Roosevelt embargoed news so that he could report back from the field himself and later write a book. There were many high points. Roosevelt killed his first lion near Mount Kilimanjaro. Bwana Makuba (Big Chief), as he was called, ate the heart of the first elephant killed, as was the custom. Over 11,000 vertebrates were killed and sorted for return, including almost 5,000 mammals. Invertebrates were also collected. Roosevelt himself killed 9 lions, 13 rhinoceroses, 7 hippopotamuses, 8 elephants, 20 zebras, 6 buffaloes, 7 giraffes, and smaller animals. In all, he had 296 kills. Kermit had 216 kills, including 8 lions. Of all the big game, Roosevelt and Kermit shared a dozen kills for trophies.

While president, Roosevelt did no writing for publication, using all his literary skills for messages and official documents. But he had not lost his talent for writing, both romantic and scientific, as his African book shows. In the foreword of his book he wrote:

> I speak of Africa and golden joys; the joy of wandering through lonely lands; the joy of hunting the mighty and terrible lords of the wilderness, the cunning, the wary, and the grim.
>
> In these greatest of the world's great hunting-grounds there are mountain peaks whose snows are dazzling under the equatorial sun; swamps where the slime oozes and bubbles and fes-

Roosevelt in British East Africa, 1909

ters in the steaming heat; lakes like seas; skies that burn above deserts where the iron desolation is shrouded from view by the wavering mockery of the mirage; vast grassy plains where palms and thorn-trees fringe the dwindling streams; mighty rivers rushing out of the heart of the continent through the sadness of endless marshes; forests of gorgeous beauty, where death broods in the dark and silent depths.

And on the pitiless death of a lion:

Right in front of me, thirty yards off, there appeared, from behind the bushes which had first screened him from my eyes, the tawny, galloping form of a big maneless lion. Crack! the Winchester spoke; and as the soft-nosed bullet ploughed forward through his flank the lion swerved so that I missed him with the second shot; but my third bullet went through the spine and forward into his chest. Down he came, sixty yards off, his hind quarters dragging, his head up, his snarl, as he endeavored to face us. His back was broken; but of this we could not at the moment be sure, and if it had merely been grazed, he might have recovered, and then, even though dying, his charge might have done mischief. So Kermit, Sir Alfred, and I fired, almost together, into his chest. His head sank, and he died.

When Roosevelt left American shores for Africa, J. P. Morgan was reported to have said in a toast, "America expects that every lion will do his duty." But the greatest lion of them all had survived.

Out of Africa in March 1910, Roosevelt immediately went on a whirlwind tour of Europe with Edith, who met her husband with Ethel in Khartoum, Sudan. The family then went to Italy, where Roosevelt had a dustup with Pope Pius X. The pontiff had invited Roosevelt to visit, but he did not wish him to also pay a call on the proselytizing and name-calling Methodists in Rome. Roosevelt resolved the dilemma by snubbing both. He visited the aging Emperor Franz Joseph I of the Austro-Hungarian empire; he trooped the colors with the boastful Emperor William II of Germany, who insisted that he pay tribute to his might; he toured Brussels and Copenhagen and was made a freeman of the city of London.

That spring, Roosevelt received an honorary degree from Cambridge University, and he gave the Romanes Lecture at Oxford University on biological analogies. His take on social Darwinism was that while biological evolution might have some guarantees, historical evolution did not. The archbishop of York graded Roosevelt with a B-minus in content and an A in performance. A less forgiving Oxford don reported that the ex-president had hit three touch points: latitude, longitude, and platitude.

Roosevelt gave his Nobel Peace Prize speech in Norway where, once more, he was a pioneer in calling for a League of Peace to prevent war (Woodrow Wilson's League of Nations and cousin Franklin Roosevelt's United Nations followed), along with a limit on naval shipbuilding and a strengthened Hague tribunal for the arbitration of disputes.

At the Sorbonne in Paris, Roosevelt summed up his philosophy:

> It is not the critic who counts. . . . The credit belongs to the man in the arena, whose face is marred by dust and sweat and blood; who strives valiantly . . . who knows the great enthusiasms, the great devotions; who spends himself in a worthy cause; who at the best knows in the end the triumph of high achievement, and who at the worst, if he fails, at least fails while daring greatly.

Roosevelt had the time of his life as a charming, natural, intelligent, and wholly representative American. He was the most famous man in the world. He took the old and stodgy European countries by storm, as they had not seen anyone like him since the Enlightenment figures Benjamin Franklin and Thomas Jefferson were on their shores.

Roosevelt's return to America on June 18, 1910, was tumultuous, and the crowd even bordered on hysterical. The largest number of people, ever, gathered in New York to greet him, and the formal ceremony had all the trappings fit for a conquering hero. Six battleships and hundreds of lesser vessels greeted Roosevelt's ship, tooting their horns in a deafening cacophony. Then a fourteen-carriage parade of notables, a regiment of Rough Riders, and a huge military band accompanied him up Broadway to Fifth Avenue.

The hunt and the European tour had affected Roosevelt, but it was this reception that made him anew. His closest associates immediately saw the change. As one put it: "He had an enlarged personality. . . . He had ceased to be an American, but had become a world citizen. His horizon seemed to be greater, his mental scope more encompassing." This was a most insightful observation, for Roosevelt would soon reenter the political arena as the indispensable leader.

Even before Roosevelt returned to America, his friends had written to him and some had even visited him abroad to tell him how badly things were going for the progressive Republican cause under Taft. Taft himself was not unaware of the turmoil in the Republican Party, which began almost from the outset of his presidency. In May 1910 he had written a plaintive letter to Roosevelt in London that he was having "a hard time governing"; he was trying to carry out Roosevelt's policies "conscientiously," but his "method of doing so has not worked out smoothly."

The canny Roosevelt summed up the situation for his best friend, Henry Cabot Lodge, about the same time: "Our own party leaders do not realize that I was able to hold the Republican party in power only because I insisted on a steady advance, and dragged them along with me." Taft had opened the ultimate Pandora's box by taking on the revision of the tariff in 1909. He supported the Payne-Aldrich tariff that lowered rates on imported goods to 38 percent, on average, from 57 percent. The rates were nearer to Democratic policy than Republican protectionism. And the devil was in the details. What southern and western farmers wanted—cheaper manufactured goods—manufacturers did not. What manufacturers wanted—cheaper resources—farmers and miners did not. And the division was also sectional, farmers and miners in the South and West versus the manufacturers in the East. Midwest Republicans, now called insurgents, protecting their sectional interests, opposed the tariff. When they allied with Democrats to revise it, Taft vetoed the effort. Roosevelt's thinking on the tariff, at this time, was that a genuinely protective measure for goods ought only to equalize the cost of labor between the United States and countries abroad. That the measure included some reforming elements like taxing corporations, did not win him over.

The president's trust policy was robust, but the rumblings that he would attempt to undo the steel trust arrangement that Roosevelt had allowed, and in effect, it seemed, had been hoodwinked into by J. P. Morgan, infuriated Roosevelt, although no action was taken until 1911. Taft was also not as protective of Roosevelt's conservation programs as expected.

In early April, however, before coming home, Roosevelt privately expressed doubts to an English friend abroad about Taft. He was "an utterly commonplace leader; good natured, feebly well meaning . . . and totally unable to grasp or put into execution any really great policy." As for himself, he was "a genuine radical" and believed in "an imperialist democracy" in the English sense. Roosevelt was mixing up American radicalism, meaning necessary, urgent change, with what he saw in Africa, that is, the English

imperialism of bringing the darker races Western civilization. It was a nonsensical pairing of countries and a tipping
of his hat toward Tory radicalism, undoubtedly to please
his English friend. But Roosevelt did not intend to jump
back into politics immediately on his return, nor did he
want to do anything to increase the divide in the Republican Party, although he sensed that his legacy was beginning to slip away.

Reinstalled in the United States, the troubled Roosevelt
began to differ with Taft, but only slowly. He had promised
to make a western speaking tour in the summer of 1910, after his return from Europe. That summer he explained
where he stood in a hastily crafted note to his son-in-law,
Congressman Nick Longworth of Ohio, whom he knew
had to stand with Taft in the coming elections:

> I feel so deeply in the necessity for what may be called "'pro-
> gressive politics." . . . Eighteen [months] ago, when Taft made
> it evident that he intended to succeed by acting in as strong a
> contrast as possible to me, I was by no means sure that he was
> not wise. . . . The last two months [he] has completely altered
> his attitude . . . [and] has seemed to want to act really along the
> lines that I acted.

He hoped that the vacillating Taft would keep on his most
recent path of holding the party together as a Roosevelt
coalition, as all prepared for the off-year elections.

Then Roosevelt shot his thunderbolt. On October 31,
1910, he publicly expressed the supreme meaning of his political career by declaring himself a full-fledged radical. He
was in Osawatomie, Kansas, the home of the executed
abolitionist John Brown, who was being memorialized as

the pre–Civil War martyr who tried to stir up a revolt to free the slaves. The ex-president wasn't interested in extolling Brown in his speech, but rather in placing the progressive movement within the Lincoln tradition.

Roosevelt gave a new name to his political program, calling it the New Nationalism. The name had been coined by Herbert Croly, a political writer whose book, *The Promise of American Life,* Roosevelt had read and admired. Croly's was a progressive tract calling for positive government in the tradition of Hamilton. Of course, Roosevelt had been practicing such active power, so it is difficult to know who was the father of the term. But he used New Nationalism as a sword, not as a body of principles. Hamilton would not have approved of his views that "the object of government is the welfare of the people"; "labor is prior to, and independent of, capital. . . . Labor is supreme. . . . Property is the fruit of labor"; "equality of opportunity" is essential; the "destruction of special privilege" is a goal; and it is important for "freemen to gain hold of the right to self government." Roosevelt would protect property, but he would not give it a vote, as it must serve and not be the master of man. In all, the ex-president thought he was reaffirming the political philosophy of the earliest Republicans and, he thought, of Abraham Lincoln, all of whom he now made progressives. What he did was to stretch Lincoln's philosophy to its outer boundaries. He was attaching heavy twentieth-century planks to a slender nineteenth-century scaffold.

Roosevelt was really only recommitting himself to a progressivism that he had been developing over the years and had actually perfected in 1907 and 1908. Regarding business and labor he called for transparency in business operations, a prohibition of corporate giving to political parties, government supervision of the capitalization of corporations, both for honesty and taxation purposes, control over "combinations," or trusts, and new powers for the Interstate Commerce Commission. He supported an income tax and an inheritance tax on large fortunes. On behalf of labor, he asked for a comprehensive workingman's compensation plan, state and national laws to regulate child labor, protection for women in the workplace, and safe and sanitary working conditions. Roosevelt made the conservation of natural resources a "moral issue." To make all these things possible, he stated that "our public men must be generally progressive."

The Osawatomie speech reinvigorated Roosevelt's progressive cohort, but it set off a torrent of horror among conservative Republicans and many of his dearest friends, like Henry Cabot Lodge. For them, property was superior to all other categories and must be protected from infringements. When Roosevelt's friends complained about his cavalier treatment of property, the perplexed ex-president held fast and retorted that he had been expounding this philosophy and program at least since 1907 or 1908. Weren't they listening?

More than ever, what Henry Adams said of Roosevelt had come to pass: "Roosevelt, more than any other man living within the age of notoriety, showed the singular primitive quality that belongs to ultimate matter—the quality that medieval theology assigned to God—pure act."

Roosevelt was the most powerful positive leader since Lincoln. He knew that rhetoric was not enough to protect progressivism. He had to reach into states and, with like-minded men, take control of the Republican Party. This led him immediately, in 1910, to entanglement in the toxic wars in New York as well as in other states between his party's progressives and conservatives. Taft was outraged, as the presumed leader of the Republicans. Roosevelt's friends were astonished by a possible coup and began backing away from him. He, himself, became disappointed. "I think we are in for a tremendous drubbing," he told Cabot. Yet the ex-president soldiered on in speeches and writings under a cloud of doom. He insisted, the Osawatomie speech notwithstanding, that he was only restating his recommendations while he was president "in precisely the spirit of Lincoln." He was more than encouraged when a *Detroit News* editorial writer, following him around, told him: "You have the greatest responsibility of any man since Lincoln."

But the Lincoln mantle Roosevelt wore for so long was becoming a tattered remnant of lost meaning to the second generation after the Civil War. History would no longer serve Roosevelt well, although he would still fly its flag. The Lincoln cloak was made of antislavery and free-labor threads. It was a garment of a strong presidency and of positive government on a national scale, favoring free homesteads, continental railroads, land-grant colleges, and a national banking system. Roosevelt extended Lincoln's political philosophy and deeds into a highly industrialized and financially sophisticated nation with extraordinary needs. The ex-president's vision of what had to be done went beyond the horizon of most Americans and almost all the political leaders in 1910. So Lincoln could no longer serve as the essential political guide except, perhaps, for his humanity. As the Federalists had given way to Jeffersonians in the early nineteenth century, Lincoln's prevailing political philosophy that replaced it was receding in the early twentieth. Roosevelt fought to keep Lincoln alive by redefining his legacy as progressivism. As in the past, however, the voters decided about the end of one era or the beginning of another.

The off-year elections in fall 1910 proved fateful for Roosevelt and for a divided Republican Party. All over the country the roar of Democrats coming back to power could be heard. Roosevelt men and the Republican Party lost in New York. On the national scene, the Democrats took control of the House for the first time in sixteen years, and the Republican majority in the Senate was whittled down. Furthermore, more than half of the governors would be Democrats.

The Theodore Roosevelt era was over in 1910. It was short, but probably the most active for reform and for change that the nation experienced up to that time. The elections showed that only about a quarter of the Republican Party was progressive. The Taft conservatives were more numerous. "We have had a smashing defeat," Roosevelt lamented. He sorrowfully mused, furthermore, that "the people were weary of Republican rule. . . . I think that the American people feel a little tired of me." More bitingly he recorded, "Well, every dog has his day; but the nights belong to the cats."

Roosevelt did not give an inch on his principles after the November debacle. He wrote in *Outlook* magazine, where he had a paid, long-standing relationship: "I have nothing whatever to add or to take away from the declaration of principles which I have made in the late Osawatomie speech and elsewhere, East and West, during the past three months. The fight for popular progressive government has merely begun." He would retreat to the shadows at Sagamore Hill.

For a time, the lion of Oyster Bay would be silent, and would enjoy the company of a loving wife and children, one of whom, Ted, was soon to make him a grandfather.

Roosevelt also had time to reflect on what is truly important in life. He summed these up in a note to Ted, Jr.:

> Home, wife, and children—they are what really count in life. I have enjoyed many things; the Presidency, my success as a soldier, a writer, a big game hunter and explorer; but all of them put together are not for one moment to be weighed in the balance when compared with the joy I have known with your mother and all of you.

Roosevelt, more than ever, found a haven within his family and on his estate. The seductive call of politics was only a whisper. His latest book, *African Game Trails*, was an enormous success and probably would earn him as much as forty thousand dollars in its first year. It verged on being a masterpiece in its genre. The younger boys were away at school, as was Ethel, unhappily. Quentin was enjoying "brilliant academic success at Groton. . . . It was almost paralyzing," Roosevelt commented. Only this youngest son was so talented academically.

Progressives would not let go of Roosevelt, however. His response to siren calls was that "they have no business to expect me to take command of a ship simply because the ship is sinking." Roosevelt expected Taft to be renominated, but La Follette badly wanted the Republican nomination. Given the fight ahead, Roosevelt expected the Democrats would win in 1912. Left standing in 1916 would be himself and La Follette, who he thought was not a major contender.

Given the political situation, as he saw it, he declared to friends that he did not want the nomination again for president in 1912. But he would make no Shermanesque statement about not running for president or not serving if elected. He no longer considered Taft his friend; rather, he called him privately "a flubdub with a streak of the second rate and the common in him." Taft soon became a "puzzle-wit" and a "fathead." Taft called Roosevelt a "demagogue."

The battle between the two giants was real and for the soul of the Republican Party. Taft wanted strict enforcement of laws against trusts in order to foster competition. He instituted more antitrust suits than the former president. Roosevelt saw size as inevitable and efficient, and he wanted only to regulate large corporations in order to make them honest. Taft tried to upend a key Roosevelt settlement in the steel industry, and Roosevelt was furious. (A later Supreme Court decision favored Roosevelt.) For Taft the judiciary was sacrosanct. Roosevelt had more than once asked for the recall of state judges who overturned social and economic reform legislation. Taft negotiated several arbitration treaties to keep peace in the world; Roosevelt thought them useless and, perhaps, dangerous documents. How could they be enforced? On labor issues, Taft got an eight-hour day for government employees and expanded the civil service. He also supported an income tax and the popular election of U.S. senators. Many of these were no different than what Roosevelt asked for.

Taft had a decent, if meager, progressive legislative record. Mostly, however, it was reactive, and Taft showed little initiative to meet progressive needs. Roosevelt men viewed him as lazy. He was said to play golf most mornings and hated too much desk work afterward. Or he was befuddled about how to lead. Roosevelt, himself, was more than disenchanted with his hand-picked successor.

Roosevelt decided that he wanted to be president again. On February 12, 1912, he offhandedly muttered to a journalist: "My hat is in the ring." That was not enough. He engineered a call from many governors asking him to run again, and he replied that he would accept the Republican nomination. La Follette had collapsed, physically, and when he returned to good health had lost his momentum. It was now Taft versus Roosevelt.

At the Ohio constitutional convention that same month, Roosevelt spoke the words that became the bedrock of his preconvention platform, and he irrevocably divided the party. He put "human rights . . . supreme over all other rights." And he said: "Wealth should be the servant, not the master of the people." In letters to him, Roosevelt learned that his close associates were now about to break from him. Elihu Root was "appalled." Lodge, with "pain," publicly broke from the politics of his old friend. He thought they had not seen eye-to-eye for at least two years, he wrote Roosevelt, and now he was "miserably unhappy" with the wide difference between them. After the parting, these two oldest of friends continued to keep in touch with each other, but their letters were rather empty, and the relationship cold. Roosevelt had strayed too far from what Root and Lodge always thought was a sensible kind of progressivism.

Roosevelt stuck to his guns. To one prominent progressive he wrote:

> [The campaign would be] a contest to establish the right of the
> people to govern themselves, and through their efforts to work

for the cause of social and industrial justice, and of good will among men ... [and] prosperity must stand on a foundation of justice, justice to the wageworker, to capitalist, to the general public.

Roosevelt's progressivism was now on a foundation of justice, no easy word to parse on the part of most Republican politicos. They had been able to deal with actual demands, but now a philosophical and undefined principle guided Roosevelt.

The genial Taft was undoubtedly traumatized by his old friend's challenge. After all, he was a sitting president pushed into office by the then wildly popular Roosevelt. Fundamentally a peaceful man, Taft had met with Roosevelt in the fall of 1910 to try to patch things up, but they left each other further apart. The two giants kept in touch, nevertheless. Roosevelt wrote to Taft about Panama, after Taft praised him, and on foreign affairs, mostly about Japan, after receiving a copy of Taft's annual message to Congress in December 1910. But the letters were straightforward and businesslike. In the summer of 1911, Roosevelt thought Taft was getting politically stronger because the Insurgents were "incoherent." He expected the president to be renominated. By fall, he wrote to Governor Hiram Johnson of California that he would support Taft if he were renominated. Cheered by the news, Taft supporters, at the end of the year, asked Roosevelt to pledge to refuse his own nomination, but Roosevelt replied that he did not want the nomination and would not make such a pledge if the nomination came to him as a "duty." No wonder Taft and his supporters, as the new year approached, had felt both bewilderment and betrayal.

In the primary elections in spring 1912, Roosevelt won nine contests, La Follette, two, and Taft, one. Reeling, Taft felt he now had to openly attack Roosevelt to regain his footing. In a fighting speech, he charged that Roosevelt was "a threat to the nation's liberty." When the president returned to his private railroad car, he told his aides that the speech was one of "the most painful duties of my life," and he put his head in his hands and wept. (He would weep again at Roosevelt's untimely death.)

All the maneuvering, invective, and conflict came to a head at the Republican convention in Chicago in June 1912, a wild affair, but not out of control. Roosevelt men tried to force the party its way and to give their leader the nomination. Roosevelt had won a majority of the Republican votes in the primaries, collecting 278 delegates to Taft's 48, and he had even beaten Taft in his home state of Ohio. But not all states had primaries. Parties chose the convention delegates in most of them, and Taft ruled in Republican state conventions, especially in the "pocket-borough delegates of the South," as Roosevelt called them. Taft's men maintained tight control of party machinery. At the convention, the national committee which ran the meeting ruled that most of Roosevelt's support consisted of contested delegates.

Roosevelt rushed to Chicago to lead the attack against the Old Guard oligarchs and their minions, who he thought could "rob" him, by denying the legitimacy of his delegates. Taft was given 235 of the contested state delegates and Roosevelt only nineteen. In all, the president

Cartoon of Roosevelt wearing his black sombrero and neckerchief from his Rough Riders days, as he wins a primary in 1912 (New Sun, April 11, 1912)

wound up with 550 delegates to Roosevelt's 450. Taft was the nominee of the Republican Party. The president had put control of the Republican Party over winning in November. After all, there would be life after 1912.

The Taft nomination was disputed ever after. Roosevelt thought Taft stole delegates and, with his supporters, bolted the convention. Historians calculate that, even if Roosevelt had won the disputed delegates, he would have lost anyway, as he still would not have commanded a majority. At best, if he had made some deals, he only would have deadlocked the convention.

Roosevelt did not take his defeat calmly. He gave a long, impassioned speech to the delegates and ended with the peroration: "We stand at Armageddon, and we battle for the Lord." The secular Roosevelt, uncharacteristically, had brought God into the political maelstrom. Taking up the religious theme, the press corps dubbed him John the Baptist.

Roosevelt men left the Republican Party and formed the Progressive Party. In August, fifteen thousand Roosevelt supporters met in Chicago to run Roosevelt for president and to write a platform. Roosevelt gave another of his memorable reformist speeches, this one called "A Confession of Faith," to an audience that seemed less like a political convention than a religious revival meeting enthralled by a charismatic preacher. Then, too, conventioneers sang "The Battle Hymn of the Republic" and "Onward, Christian Soldiers" with religious fervor.

There was a downside to the injection of God and religion at the Progressives' meeting. One nasty, anonymous circular announced that Roosevelt would soon be walking on water at Lake Michigan.

Roosevelt's "Confession" restated his progressivism, widely known since his Osawatomie speech. He mentioned his social and economic goals, and he added to them giving "a living wage" for workers, an incredibly advanced position not honored even today. Large businesses needed to be regulated so that there would be decent prices and wages. A tariff ought to benefit consumers and laborers. The currency system needed improvement so that it would be more flexible and responsive to the needs of both business and producers like farmers and miners.

Roosevelt added that an efficient army and growing navy were essential. Judges should be recalled if they rejected social and economic reforms. Conservation of the nation's natural resources should be continued.

The "Confession" also included many of the new demands of western, and some eastern, progressives. These were national presidential primaries; the direct election of U.S. senators, taking away the power from the states, as the Constitution provided; the initiative to give voters a way to put laws on the books when state legislatures would not; a referendum for voters to accept or reject state legislation; and women's suffrage. The speech was long and professorial, detailed and lacking in fire. But almost all these "western" demands came to pass within a generation.

During the election, Roosevelt took on the Democratic nominee, Woodrow Wilson, whom he thought his biggest adversary, relegating Taft to a supporting role, along with Eugene V. Debs, the candidate of the Socialist Party.

The most eventful happening in the 1912 campaign was that Roosevelt was shot by an unknown assailant in October. The bullet went through his coat, steel eyeglass case, and a thick manuscript. It pierced four inches into his chest, breaking a rib and lodging against it. Falling back, Roosevelt determined that, because he was not spitting up blood, the bullet had missed his lung. He would proceed with his speech. "It was a perfectly obvious duty," to go on, he later explained to a friend. He decided that "in the very unlikely event of the wound being mortal I wished to die with my boots on."

Roosevelt informed his audience that he had been shot and would not be able to speak loudly, and he held forth for about an hour and a half in hushed tones. He was then

Roosevelt, the Progressive Party
candidate for President, 1912

rushed to the hospital. Ever ebullient, Roosevelt did not take the episode too seriously and quipped to Cabot and his wife in a letter, "I feel like the old maid who, when she at last discovered a man under the bed, seized him and said: 'You're the burglar I have been looking for these last twenty years.'" Clearly, presidential politics had become more dangerous to Roosevelt than the war in Cuba, where he suffered only a glancing bullet to his elbow. With his courageous demeanor, another heroic deed was added to the Roosevelt mythology.

Roosevelt's tumultuous campaign and near death could not save him. The old soldier came in second, behind Wilson. Roosevelt's showing was a last great tribute to the nation's greatest living hero. When the election was over, he commented to friends in letters:

> We have fought the good fight, we have kept the faith . . . and we have nothing to repent.

> I feel horribly at not being President.

> The Progressive movement must and will go forward even though its progress is fitful. . . . The alternative is oscillation between the greedy arrogance of a party directed by conscienceless millionaires and the greedy envy of a party directed by reckless and unscrupulous demagogues.

Roosevelt seemed to know that the progressive phase within the Republican Party was ended, although he hoped the cause would yet survive in the new organization.

The defeated Roosevelt was more specific in his calculations and hopes in a letter to Charles Dwight Willard on November 14:

> Of course I would greatly have preferred if we could have made the Republican Party a Progressive party, such as it was when founded by Lincoln, even such as it was when I was in the White House. . . . Then even if defeated this year we would have had one strong progressive party in opposition. . . .

I have not one regret. . . . At the moment our task is to try to make the progressive party a strong permanent organization.

Progressivism did not survive in the Republican Party. The Progressive Party limped along. Roosevelt had transformed the measured radicalism of Lincoln into a modern idiom in 1912, and they both lost.

Roosevelt retreated into his private life after the epochal 1912 election. He wrote his autobiography, to be published in 1913. In it, he was informative, if not reflective, and made few judgments, so he left out events that he perceived as unflattering, like the Brownsville incident when black troopers were involved in a melee, a white man died, and Roosevelt dismissed the whole company. Still, the account gives great detail about his family roots and political life. Glorious details about how he entered politics, his rise and plans, his soldiering, and his philosophy of governing, which was more practical than ideological, are all unmatched compared with the writings of other presidents. The volume is quietly defensive of an extraordinary life lived in several worlds. It is what Roosevelt wanted future public men to learn from, if they were daring enough. It was here he put meat on the bones of two of his most memorable statements, made in 1899: "The virtue that is worth having is the virtue that can sustain the rough shock of actual living." "Evil cannot be done away with through one spasm of virtue."

During these months, Roosevelt also kept up with his journalistic articles on topical subjects. Then he accepted invitations rejected earlier to lecture in South America. With Edith for part of the trip, Roosevelt visited several countries, among them Brazil, Chile, and Argentina. In his lectures, the traveler suggested an evolutionary philosophic change to the Roosevelt corollary of the Monroe Doctrine—an astonishing multilateralism. He suggested that it might be possible for large and vital countries of South America, like some he was visiting, to help police the Monroe Doctrine. "As soon as any country of the New World stands on a sufficiently high footing of orderly liberty and achieved success, of self-respecting strength," he said, "it becomes a guarantor of the doctrine on a footing of complete equality." Roosevelt had been unwilling, until now, to share power with Caribbean powers. He had always recognized European balance-of-power politics. Of course, he had no choice in the latter case, but he didn't have to take a liberal stance. As he and the republics of the South matured, he looked to multipolar solutions to problems. It was a futuristic vision that would not be realized until his cousin Franklin Roosevelt was president.

Writing, speechmaking, keeping the Progressives united, and traveling were not enough to tame Roosevelt's still-bursting energy. In the fall of 1913, he returned to combat in nature's wars. The intrepid explorer ventured into the Brazilian jungle, staying away for about nine months. Roosevelt trekked into a heart of darkness with his redoubtable son, Kermit, and a score of men to engage in scientific work for the American Museum of Natural History. The ex-president mapped the longest river after the Rhine and Elbe and, perhaps, the fiercest unexplored wild river—the 1500-mile River of Doubt, later called Rio Roosevelt—north of the Amazon. Always writing, Roosevelt later published an engaging book on the expedition,

Through the Brazilian Jungle, which quickly made him the equivalent of his annual salary as president.

But there was an almost fatal side to this adventure. Roosevelt caught malaria and had dysentery. He injured a leg that became infected and caused a raging 105-degree fever. He was so sick that, in one version of this journey, he contemplated suicide and asked Kermit to leave him behind so as not to impede the effort to get out of the raging waters. Ultimately, he decided not to give up, writing that "it is [a man's] duty to go forward, if necessary on all fours, until he drops." Roosevelt lost fifty-seven pounds from the struggle—in his Cuban adventure he had lost only twenty—and he remained debilitated for some time. He never wholly recovered his robust health, and germs lay hidden in his compromised body.

Roosevelt returned home in May 1914 to neither drums nor trumpets. He had become a private citizen at last. But world events would not allow him to stay at home with his books, family, and comforts. The guns of August 1914 boomed out war in Europe. Not since Napoleon's imperialist actions a hundred years before had war on such a scale and horror visited Europe. Many of the antagonisms Roosevelt had striven so hard and successfully to mediate as president quickly exploded. He could not contain himself, as he witnessed Germany's belligerent behavior and warmongering. Roosevelt lacked confidence in President Wilson to manage international affairs, referring to him in private letters as "a prize jackass." He likened Wilson to Jefferson and Madison, who he believed were excessively pacific. Because of their lack of preparedness, he charged, Madison had allowed the country to be invaded by England in 1812 and the White

House to be burned. Of the three political parties, only the Progressive Party favored measures for preparedness, surely a tribute to Roosevelt for whom preparedness meant the hope for peace and the certainty of victory in war.

The off-year elections of 1914 reflected the peaceful predilections of the majority of Americans, however, and they shattered the Progressive Party. Progressive candidates, except in California, were defeated. Roosevelt was not downcast, but he thought the reform impulse was dead. He would continue to enjoy a private life.

In the summer of 1914, Germany invaded the small brave nation of Belgium, whose neutrality was protected by a Hague treaty. The kaiser wrote to Roosevelt hoping he would gain his support, but the ex-president, who was always wary of William II, would not nod his way.

President Wilson thought it his duty to follow public opinion and not lead it, in staunch opposition to Roosevelt's presidential proclivities. Then Roosevelt gave his verdict that justice was on invaded Belgium's side. Had he been president, he would have looked to the Hague treaty, which guaranteed Belgium's neutrality, and he would have been willing to back up the guarantee with war against the aggressor. Certainly by the winter of 1915, Roosevelt tended to favor an American entry into the war on the side of the Allies, but he thought there was, as yet, no casus belli.

But then, on May 6, 1915, the world turned upside down and went spinning sideways with the horrific sinking of the Cunard liner *Lusitania* by a German U-boat. Eleven hundred people drowned, including 124 Americans. The British boat was unarmed but was carrying war materiel. It had been caught in a crossfire when the Germans were trying to end the war quickly by denying England food and supplies. England had blockaded the continental coast to deny Germany food and materials, and this deadly act was the aggressor's response. Wilson sent a stern note to Germany, demanding, among other things, reparations for the lost Americans, which he received. He continued to hope for a negotiated peace to end the war. By contrast, Roosevelt, who believed that neutral rights should be protected, had found his casus belli.

As usual, Roosevelt was most truculent in his private correspondence against Wilson's peaceful stance, calling him "that infernal skunk in the White House." On a more literary level, he wrote at length to Cecil Spring Rice: "Untried men who live at ease will do well to remember that there is a certain sublimity even in Milton's defeated archangel, but none whatever in the spirits who kept neutral." When he wrote to a journalist friend in the same vein, the friend responded that the ex-president ought to take to attacking literary giants and not the giants of the Democratic Party, meaning Wilson and Bryan, the most vocal pacifist in the country.

Roosevelt also wrote searing articles later published in 1915 as *America and the World War*. In these he attacked Wilson and called Secretary of the Navy Josephus Daniels incompetent.

Wilson continued his policy of neutrality while holding the Germans to what he called "strict accountability." But the White House "accountant," the name given Wilson by his Republican adversaries, waited months before asking Congress for money to prepare the country for any eventuality. His stance was summed up in his statement that "there is such a thing as a man being too proud to fight."

When Wilson finally addressed the American people, however, he sounded like Roosevelt when he asked for the largest and most comprehensive program ever for naval expansion. Taking other pages from Roosevelt's playbook, Wilson laid the groundwork for a negotiated settlement from a position of strength while defending America's worldwide interests. Roosevelt, however, judged Wilson's effort as falling short of the mark, for he had not asked for enough money to build an effective army.

Roosevelt dearly missed not being president during this greatest crisis in the world during his lifetime. Here was a chance to relive the Civil War and to be Abraham Lincoln. By 1916 he gave up the Progressive Party, his friends bitterly charging him with a betrayal of principles and the killing of their organization. But Roosevelt knew a lost cause when he saw one, and he now badly wanted the upcoming Republican nomination for president. There wasn't a chance he could get it, given his bolt, the animus of the old guard, and the break with his closest Republican friends, some of whom were power brokers in the party, like Root. At their convention, Republicans gave Roosevelt an ovation of thirty-six minutes, the longest at the meeting, but it led nowhere. The party was bestowing love and not power. The tightly controlled Republicans nominated the reformist New York Governor Charles Evans Hughes as their candidate. Roosevelt was angry and concluded that the nation was not "in a heroic mood."

In a thoughtful moment, Roosevelt declared that he had made a mistake in 1912. Had he not left the Republican Party he could have had the nomination. Yet, he ultimately accepted Hughes, a man he privately described as the "bearded lady" and a "cold fish." In private, Roosevelt thought the Republicans who chose Hughes better people than the Democrats who renominated Wilson. In his inimitable words, Republicans were "a trifle better than the corrupt and lunatic wild asses of the desert." Roosevelt did not lash out publicly after his rejection, but sensibly—at least if he wanted a political future—spent his time excoriating Wilson and pacifists.

Roosevelt stumped for Hughes and imitated loyalty to the Republican Party. The cold fish lost the election, although narrowly. Roosevelt calculated that it was because he was not progressive enough and he lacked vision, the latter a necessary commodity for presidential success. Wilson's pacific campaign was based on the statement "He Kept Us out of War," and it succeeded all too well.

When the Germans announced unrestricted submarine warfare in January 1917, sinking three American ships, among others, Roosevelt thought war inevitable, even though the president merely broke off relations with Germany. Another bizarre event also impelled Wilson's action—the discovery of the soon-to-be-infamous Zimmermann telegram. Germany offered a deal to Mexico: a Frenchman would be put on the Mexican throne and California, Arizona, and New Mexico would be returned to it, if Mexico pledged to invade the United States.

Then Roosevelt stopped attacking Wilson because he needed him for his plan to get into the war. He asked the secretary of war for permission to form a regiment to fight in France. When he did not get a positive answer, he went to see Wilson in the White House. The president did not like Roosevelt and bitterly resented his personal attacks. Yet, to his surprise, Wilson found Roosevelt a sweet-tempered man, and he was almost beguiled. But the president stood firm against the old soldier for many good reasons, including the fact that the army did not want him. It had become a professionalized fighting force and could not accommodate Roosevelt's volunteers. The war was a desperate and huge struggle against large and modernized armies—often tens of thousands of men died in a single battle—and a Roosevelt-ian cavalry charge or skirmish up a hill was not what was needed. Roosevelt was more than disappointed, and he let it be known that if he could go to war in France, he expected he would never return. The witty Elihu Root teased, "If Wilson were assured of that, permission . . . to go overseas would be immediately forthcoming."

On April 17, just before Roosevelt's visit, Wilson asked Congress for a declaration of war. The next year, Roosevelt put himself through a strenuous war bond tour, buying sixty thousand dollars worth of bonds himself, using almost all of his cash. Many times on his hustings, he showed an unacceptable intolerance toward German Americans, dissent, and the free press. It was another black moment in the Roosevelt story.

Three of Roosevelt's sons were soon in the fight. Two of these boys became decorated heroes. The youngest and most promising, Quentin, was "the last of the lion's brood" to go to war, as his father put it. Roosevelt rejoiced with Quentin when he was blooded in a dogfight, but the youngster was killed in a fight over Germany. When his body was identified as Roosevelt's son, the kaiser ordered him buried with full military honors.

Once more, the light went out of Roosevelt's life, and Edith was inconsolable. Roosevelt took up his pen to eulogize fallen soldiers:

Only those are fit to live who do not fear to die; and none are fit to die who have shrunk from the joy of life and the duty of life. Both life and death are parts of the same Great Adventure. . . . Unless men are willing to fight and die for great ideals, including love of country, ideals will vanish, and the world will become one huge sty of materialism. . . . All of us who give service, and stand ready for sacrifice, are the torchbearers. . . . The torches whose flames are brightest are borne by the gallant men at the front. . . . These are the torchbearers; these are they who have dared the Great Adventure.

Roosevelt had hoped that Germany would be made to surrender unconditionally, as he saw trouble ahead with an armistice and Wilson's "peace without victory" in November 1918. The Allies behaved as though they had won the war, and Wilson led peace efforts by proposing fourteen points for a settlement, including the formation of a League of Nations to keep the peace. The document was an ultranationalistic statement that broke up two old empires—the Austro-Hungarian and the Ottoman—into small, self-identified nation-states. The league substituted a multinational overlord organization for individual nation-state power in international affairs.

Wilson made the 1918 off-year elections on November 5 a test of voters' confidence in his leadership. He did not get it. In a remarkable repudiation, the two houses of Congress went Republican, by twenty-one seats in the House and two in the Senate. Still, Wilson sailed to France on December 3 to engage in peace-treaty activity based, mostly, on his fourteen points. No member of the Senate was included in Wilson's peace task force, and only one so-called

Republican, Henry White—Roosevelt called him an "Independent"—a diplomat and skilled mediator, went along.

When Wilson presented the Versailles Treaty to the
Senate for ratification, Henry Cabot Lodge opposed it
and presented reservations against some of its articles,
particularly the League of Nations. A strong nationalist,
he was not going to have a foreign combine tell the
United States how to behave in foreign affairs. Roosevelt
kept track of Wilson's peace proposals, and he wrote articles with his views in the *Kansas City Star* on October 17
and 30, 1918. He found Wilson's fourteen points "muddy,"
"incomprehensible," and "very treacherous." The League
of Nations he thought "akin to the holy alliance of the
nations of Europe a century ago." (The Holy Alliance
had put Europe back together again after the Napoleonic
wars.) Roosevelt argued that "if it is designed to do away
with nationalism, it will work nothing but mischief." He
also thought the fourteen points would limit tariffs,
threaten national security with its disarmament inclu-
sions, and foster a "freedom of the seas" that would assist
"aggressors," among other points. He added that he
would not use the army in any "obscure fights" or "in a
war we do not approve of."

Roosevelt continued to be skeptical about the League
of Nations as the weeks went by. His last statement, before
he died, was written for the *Kansas City Star* and was dated
January 3, 1919, and published ten days later: "We all
earnestly desire such a league, only we wish to be sure that
it will help and not hinder the course of world peace and
justice." He suggested that each nation must clearly set
forth questions that were "non-justiciable," and that nothing "will interfere with our preparing for [our] own defense

by introducing a system of universal obligatory military training modelled on the Swiss plan." Wilson was obdurate on any change, however, and the Versailles Treaty was rejected by the Senate.

There was some talk of giving Roosevelt the 1920 Republican nomination, after the stunning victory of the party in 1918. Back home at Christmas, after a hospital stay for terrible illnesses, Roosevelt was at peace with himself. His last remembered words were, "I wonder if you will ever know how I love Sagamore Hill."

On January 6, 1919, Edith was called into Roosevelt's sick room in early morning by the ex-president's caretaker, who was worried about his rattled breathing. Seeing her stricken husband, Edith wailed, "Theodore darling, Theodore darling." Archie, at home recovering from his war wounds, sent a simple cable to his brothers: "The old lion is dead."

Acknowledgments

❧ THIS SHORT BIOGRAPHY IS BASED ALMOST entirely on the abundant printed primary and secondary sources on Theodore Roosevelt and his era. First, and foremost, is the 8-volume selection of Roosevelt's *Letters*, from among the 150,000 missives he left us, edited by Elting E. Morison, John Morton Blum, and Alfred D. Chandler, Jr. (Cambridge: Harvard University Press, 1951–54). The editors appended incisive essays on aspects of Roosevelt's life and work to these letters. The collection is a remarkable treasure trove that brings Roosevelt to life. Second, is the 20-volume collection of Roosevelt's writings, *The National Edition of Roosevelt's Works*, published by Charles Scribner's Sons in 1926. These volumes include all his books, articles, essays, and occasional writings, with various valuable prefaces and essays by editors and historians. Third, there are at least a half dozen superb, long biographies of Roosevelt that I consulted with enormous profit. These include *The Rise of Theodore Roosevelt* (New York: Modern Library, 2001) and *Theodore Rex* (New York: Random

House, 2001) by Edmund Morris; *Theodore Roosevelt: A Life* by Nathan Miller (New York: Morrow, 1992); *TR: The Last Romantic* by H. W. Brands (New York: Basic Books, 1997); and *Theodore Roosevelt: A Strenuous Life* by Kathleen Dalton (New York: Alfred A. Knopf, 2002). Fourth and finally, there are dozens of books on numerous aspects of Roosevelt's life and times that provide insight.

All the letters and writings referred to in the text are from the printed editions of his *Letters* or *Works* and can easily be found by their dates or by their titles. I am grateful to all the scholars who came before me for their dedicated work.

I want to acknowledge the help of a number of people who made this work a joyful experience by their interest and concern. My husband, the historian David Herbert Donald, is my great champion. He read an early version of the work, called it excellent, and suggested—while offering advice—that I prepare it for publication for a general audience. His encouragement carried me forward. Two friends with Harvard University Press connections also inspired me at a crucial stage. They are Virginia La Plante and Susan Wallace Boehmer. Each suggested how I could make the book a more engaging study. In his spare time, Ian Stevenson, of Harvard University Press, was my research assistant in gathering up the Roosevelt illustrations. I thank Wallace Dailey, Curator of the Theodore Roosevelt Collection at the Houghton Library of Harvard University, for his attentive and excellent help with the illustrations.

At an early stage of my work, my friend Morton Keller gave me his set of the Roosevelt *Letters* that eased my research immeasurably. At about the same time, my husband gave me a set of Roosevelt's *Works* one Christmas. Both gifts allowed me to read through the volumes in the comfort of my study in Lincoln. Over the years, Phyllis Keller and Sonia and David Landes showed gracious interest in this book.

I owe immeasurable gratitude to my editor at Basic Books, Lara Heimert, for her almost boundless enthusiam for the biography and invaluable editorial help. I will always treasure her friendship. I owe heartfelt thanks to Kay Mariea, Director of Editorial Services, and Tom Lacey, my copy editor, at Perseus Books Group. Matt Seccombe read the proof with great care. I owe a debt to my indexer Donna Riggs. Kristi Stone helped with computer problems and made my knowledge of this new way of writing a pleasure.

I want to thank Jill Marsal and Taryn Fagerness of the Sandra Dijkstra Literary Agency for their help, and Sandy herself, my friend of almost 35 years, for her skillful interest in my book. My dear friend, Dr. Vivian Sanchez, was a life-saver at a critical juncture in the publishing journey of my book.

For all the help I received, I should be offering a perfect book; for any errors, I am alone responsible.

Index